A CONTEMPLATIVE READING OF THE GOSPEL

Mark

The Risk of Believing

By Elena Bosetti

Pauline

BOOKS & MEDIA

Boston

Library of Congress Cataloging-in-Publication Data

Bosetti, Elena.
  [Marco. English]
  Mark : the risk of believing / Elena Bosetti. — 1st English ed.
     p. cm.
  ISBN 0-8198-4847-6 (pbk.)
  1. Bible. N.T. Mark—Criticism, interpretation, etc. 2. Faith. 3. Belief and doubt.
I. Title.
  BS2585.6.F3B6713 2006
  226.3'06—dc22

                              2006025644

Cover design by Rosana Usselmann

Cover art: Saint Mark: Gospels of the Cisoing Abbey, mid-twelfth century, France. Bridgeman-Giraudon / Art Resource, NY.

"P" and PAULINE are registered trademarks of the Daughters of St. Paul.

English language edition arranged through the mediation of Eulama Literary Agency

Original edition published in Italian under the title *Marco: Il rischio di credere*

Translated by Julia Mary Darrenkamp, FSP

Copyright © 2000 Centro Editoriale Dehoniano, Bologna

First English edition, 2006

Published by Pauline Books & Media, 50 Saint Paul's Avenue, Boston, MA 02130-3491. www.pauline.org

Printed in the U.S.A.

Pauline Books & Media is the publishing house of the Daughters of St. Paul, an international congregation of women religious serving the Church with the communications media.

1 2 3 4 5 6 7 8 9   11 10 09 08 07 06

To my brothers,
Tullio and Claudio

Contents

PART I

"Do you see something?"
A Journey to See

PART II

"Come after me"

A Journey to Follow

Preface

*I*s there still room for adventure on our planet? Are we still fascinated by different worlds, faraway lands, and thrilling destinations? It would certainly seem so, looking at the thriving business that travel agencies do today.

But to be a real traveler it's not enough merely to go on a trip; nor can one call oneself a true pilgrim simply by signing up for a pilgrimage. Some people travel and no longer know how to marvel at life; others make pilgrimages and don't appreciate the effort necessary for such a journey.

Something similar could be said for those making a spiritual journey or pilgrimage through life. Today more than ever people lack the patience to take one step after another. No one has time any more. Distances disappear thanks to always faster means of transportation and communication. And perhaps this fools us into believing that it should be as easy to arrive at our spiritual goals.

How can we undertake the way of the Messiah on the pathways of our time? The itinerary I would like to propose will be provided by a sometimes uncomfortable guide, the evangelist Mark. He will oblige us to rediscover the Christian vocation by climbing up the *archè* again—that is, starting at the beginning and foundation of the Gospel: the person of Jesus the Messiah, the Son of God.

In the first part of this book, *A Journey to See,* we will read the Gospel of Mark from a particular perspective. Throughout Mark's account a strong narrative tension exists between those who literally cannot see, those who know how to see but don't, and those who do not want to see. Then there is Jesus, who gives sight to the blind, questions those who say they can "see," and asks of his disciples the courage to follow him in order to see *beyond.* Faith is a journey that brings us to the point of seeing what we would rather not: God on the cross. It is a journey we must be willing to begin again, even after having committed the greatest personal failure. To the disciples who had abandoned him and to Peter who had denied him, the Risen Christ sent word: "Go to Galilee; there you will see me."

In the second part of the book, *A Journey to Follow,* we will delve into four dynamic attitudes necessary for discipleship: faith, prayer, announcement, and poverty. Discipleship means letting ourselves be formed in the school of Jesus Christ and following him on his way, making our own his sentiments of faith in the Father and compassion for the multitudes hungry for the Word of God. Christ's way unfolds from Galilee to Jerusalem. It is a way of love that liberates, heals, and gives life.

In making this journey together, my wish is that we too will be able to see beyond; that we too will be able to take the risk of believing.

Introduction

A fascinating account

*T*he Gospel of Mark has had a strange destiny. Remaining on the outskirts of exegesis for centuries (in fact, until the Second Vatican Council, only four passages of Mark besides the account of the Passion appeared during the whole cycle of liturgical readings), today Mark's Gospel has captured the limelight: it is the Gospel most interpreted by scholars and the one preferred by catechists.

Mark's account holds the reader in suspense from beginning to end. Its dramatic force was confirmed by a theatrical group that by now has traveled all over the world. In 1978, the actor Alec McCowen recited the Gospel of Mark from beginning to end on a deliberately bare stage. The simple recitation of text—without deletions, additions, or touch-ups of any kind—succeeded in captivating audiences, conveying an overall impression of a dramatic work in every respect.

So the question spontaneously arises: Was this Gospel (the shortest, at under 12,000 words) written precisely in order to be read from beginning to end in one sitting—at

least during the night of the Easter Vigil? There are scholars (such as B. Standaert) who support this view, maintaining that Mark would be a good example of *haggadah
pasquale cristiana* (in Hebrew, *haggadah* means story and
refers to a text read during the Passover seder that recounts
the story of the Exodus). According to these scholars,
Mark was developed as a liturgical story particularly
addressed to the catechumen who would be baptized during the Easter Vigil.

Perhaps this is only a quaint hypothesis. The fact
remains, however, that Mark's account comes across as a
strong and attractive narrative. While it certainly can't
compete with Luke's refined elegance, it has a lively style,
at times picturesque and attentive to detail. A characteristic of Marcan language is the use of numerous *Latinisms*:
Latin words simply transliterated into Greek. They had to
have been words that were rather well diffused in the
Mediterranean region—for example, certain political-mil-
itary terms (such as "tribute," Mk 12:14; "legion," 5:9; and
"centurion," 15:39, 44) and other commonly used words.
Mark also frequently makes use of Aramaic terms, but
these are unfailingly translated into Greek: a mark of
attention toward his intended audience, who didn't know
the language that Jesus spoke.

But there is another aspect to Mark that strikes me.
The Gospel story ends abruptly, with the silence of the
women at the tomb. The tension that has been created by
everything that happened on the cross goes unresolved.
After the crucifixion, the narrative continues with the

Easter announcement, the good news reserved to the women: "Do not be alarmed, you are looking for Jesus the Nazarene who was crucified; he is risen, he is not here..." (Mk 16:6). This announcement is accompanied by a mission: "...Go tell his disciples and Peter, 'He is going ahead of you into Galilee; you will see him there just as he told you'" (Mk 16:7).

Yet the women leave the sepulcher in a hurry and strangely say "nothing to anyone because they were afraid" (Mk 16:8). And this is how Mark ends his story. As a matter of fact, the text that follows (16:9–20) is commonly held to be an appendix to the Gospel account. Mark does not recount any "apparitions" of the Risen Christ. The ending is simply the handing on of a promise: "Go to Galilee; there you will see him."

Surprisingly Mark, from beginning to end. He always shows Jesus going ahead, always "in front of." Just when you think you've caught up with him, or that you are beginning to understand him, you realize that he is actually "beyond" you, elusive as always. Jesus goes ahead, calling us irresistibly to follow him.

Who is Mark?

The most ancient testimony we have about the person and activity of this evangelist has been handed down by Eusebius of Caesarea (*Hist. Eccl. III*, 38, 14–15), who cites Papias of Hierapolis (*Logion Kyriakon exegesis*, A.D. 120–130). In his turn, Papias takes us back to the very declarations he would have heard from the presbyter John. Here is the testimony:

> The presbyter used to hear that Mark, having been the interpreter [*hermêneutês*] of Peter, wrote with care [*akribôs egrapsen*], even though without order, all that he remembered of the sayings and facts of the Lord.
>
> He had not personally heard or followed the Lord, but Peter; and that occurred much later, as I have said. Peter taught according to the circumstances, without giving any order to the sayings [*logia*] of the Lord. However, Mark did not commit any errors in writing according to what he remembered. He had only one concern: not to omit anything of what he had heard and to relate nothing false (*Hist. Eccl. III,* 39, 15).

Among the most ancient texts that speak of the Gospels, there exists a Latin prologue dating from the second half of the second century, "Against the Marcionites" (so-called because it opposed the heresy of Marcion, which not only refuted the Old Testament, but also the Gospels of Matthew and John). In this prologue we read the following testimony:

> Here are the statements of Mark, nicknamed *the man of short fingers* [*colobodactylus*] because, despite the appearance of his stature, his fingers were too short; he was Peter's translator. After Peter's death he put into writing this Gospel in Italy.

For others, however, the phrase "man of short fingers" means that he wrote a short Gospel.

The Mark-Peter connection was constantly reprised in successive traditions, until St. Jerome composed his brilliant formula: *"Petro narrante et illo scribente"* (Peter narrated and he [Mark] wrote).

According to Eusebius of Caesarea (*Hist. Eccl. II*, 15, 2), whose writings referred to Clement of Alexandria and Papias of Hierapolis, the editing of the Gospel occurred during the lifetime of Peter, who would have "authorized the writing for reading in the Church." For other Fathers, instead, Mark would have written the Gospel after the Apostle's martyrdom, with the intention of putting in writing all that he remembered of Peter's preaching. In both cases, Mark's direct connection to the figure of Peter is the important element. According to tradition, Mark was the evangelizer of Alexandria, Egypt, where he was eventually martyred.

A mediating figure

Witnesses of the early Church tended to couple the tradition relating to John Mark of Jerusalem, companion of Paul and Barnabas in their first missionary journey, with that of Mark the "son" of Peter, who resided in "Babylon" —that is, in Rome (1 Pt 5:13).

In the Acts of the Apostles, Mark emerges as a figure of mediation: he has a connection with Peter as well as with Paul, the two apostles who most represented the early evangelization to the Hebrews and Gentiles respectively.

In Acts 12 we hear that after Peter's miraculous liberation from prison, he seeks refuge in the house of Mary, "the mother of John who is called Mark" (v. 12). This is the first time Mark is mentioned in the New Testament. By the end of the passage (v. 25) he is already associated to Barnabas and Paul, who take him along as a companion and collaborator on their first missionary journey (cf. Acts 13:5). But for some unknown reason, Mark separates from them and returns to Jerusalem (cf. Acts 13:5–13). Afterward, Paul refuses to bring him along on the second missionary journey, thereby provoking disagreement with and separation from Barnabas, who was Mark's cousin (cf. Acts 15:37–39).

We encounter Mark's name again among the few collaborators Paul mentions during his Roman imprisonment. Here the Apostle recommends that Mark be welcomed warmly by the community in Colossae (Col 4:10); and on another occasion Paul asks him to come, finding him very "useful to me in the ministry" (2 Tm 4:11). On one hand, therefore, John Mark can be described as a collaborator of Paul. Initially indecisive, Mark later became a man of faith whom the Apostle Paul could send as his spokesman to the churches in the East (Col 4:10). On the other hand, there is Mark, "son" of Peter (1 Pt 5:13), Peter's faithful interpreter and precise editor of the Gospel.

By now the presence of Peter and Paul in Rome, where both will undergo martyrdom, seems undeniable. And perhaps this is actually the reason for the traditional identification of Mark, companion of Paul, with Mark, son of Peter (1 Pt 5:13).

This brief presentation allows us to glimpse something interesting about the kind of Christianity (and theology) that came to assert itself in Rome around the years 60–70. This Christianity is capable of integrating different traditions, both Pauline and Petrine, and, more widely, the Judaic-Palestinian traditions with the traditions developed in the Diaspora and in the missions to the Gentiles.

Mark doesn't say why or for whom he wrote the Gospel; this is something one has to glean from reading the text. It is generally held that the Gospel was written for Christians coming from pagan backgrounds. But our evangelist, being a bridge between Peter and Paul, would have been able to think of an audience coming from both sides. In Rome there would have to have been different "domestic churches" (private homes where Christians would gather for worship prior to the construction of churches), comprised of Christians more of ethnic than of Judaic origins (cf. Rm 16). And in the Gospel of Mark we find Jesus' identity proclaimed both by Jews (e.g., Peter, Bartimaeus) and by pagans/Romans (the centurion beneath the cross).

A late success

The "success" of Mark's Gospel began with the discovery of its precedence. In 1938, two Germans, C. H. Weisse and C. C. Wilke, who were coming from different approaches, ended up with the same result: Mark's antecedence over Matthew and Luke. Some decades after these studies, H. J. Holzmann confirmed the hypothesis that in the complex relationship existing between the

Synoptic Gospels, Mark had been the "font" rather than merely an unoriginal abbreviation of Matthew, as St. Augustine had believed.

After the Second World War, the merit of having established the gospel as a literary genre was also recognized. Besides being the first chronologically, Mark would also be the author of an original kerygmatic project. For the first time, what was eminently an oral activity (*evangelization*) took written form, giving origin to that singular story that we call "Gospel."

Before Mark, there existed verbal accounts (*logia*) of parables and miracles. Collections of various material, they were as yet an unorganized collection of sayings and facts about Jesus, his ministry, the reasons for his death, and his messianic identity.

Today it is commonly held that Mark is not merely a simple "compiler" of diverse material (miracles, controversies, parables...), but an author in the fullest sense of the word, and one with his own particular theology. We could characterize it as divine power revealed in the greatest weakness, the theology of the glorious cross. It is the theology we find in the first Letter of Paul to the Corinthians, but also in the First Letter of Peter. Our evangelist fully grasps the identity of the Messiah and of his God on the cross.

Mark's account allows one to enter into precise space and time coordinates without remaining imprisoned by them. His Gospel finds in the liturgy an ideal ambiance for proclamation and the response of faith. The Gospel's "open-ended" conclusion, perhaps intentionally left incomplete, suggests that the evangelist intends to involve his listeners so that they continue the story—in their own lives.

PART I

"Do you see something?"

A Journey to See

I'd like to begin by looking at a curious detail in Mark's account of the passion, a detail that temporarily diminishes the dramatic tension underlying Christ's capture. We are inside the Garden of Gethsemane. Jesus, betrayed by one of his most intimate friends, now finds himself in the hands of his enemies. All of his disciples have fled in panic. But a boy gives proof of his courage. This intrepid young man succeeded in escaping the watchful care of his parents; now, under the spring's full moon (we are close to Passover), he doesn't go unobserved by the guards. The boy emerges from behind the olive trees, wrapped in a sheet, and they immediately seize him. With agile acrobatics, he manages to wiggle out from under the material enfolding him and tears away, leaving his improvised garment in the guards' hands.

Only Mark records this episode, which has all the flavor of a personal memory, a boy's act of bravado. The evangelist, by now advanced in years, must have smiled at recalling such an adventure. But perhaps there is more to the incident. If Mark lingers on this detail at such an intense narrative moment as that of Jesus' capture, perhaps it is so that we may grasp a symbolic aspect of the story. On one hand, the youth resembles Jesus, since like the Master he was "taken" (cf. Mk 14:44–45, 51); on the other hand, he flees the scene just like the disciples. He wants to see, but seems to be attracted more out of curiosity than out of love. In fact, he prefers to escape naked rather than follow the Master: he is not yet ready to lose his life.

This detail takes on a symbolic note if one reads it within the context of the end of Mark's Gospel. On the morning after the Sabbath, when the women go to the tomb with the intention of anointing the body of their beloved Master with aromatic perfume, they find inside "a youth" (*neaniskos,* the same word used in Mk 14:51) dressed in a white robe. "Don't be alarmed," he says, "you are looking for Jesus the Nazarene who was crucified; he is risen, he is not here" (16:5–6). Only Mark speaks of a *neaniskos* inside the tomb, thus creating a link—at least a literary one—with the youth at Gethsemane. But perhaps a playful symbolism is at work as well: Has the young man who escaped naked now found his clothes again?

These two young men, the one at Gethsemane and the one on Easter morning, reclothe themselves in symbolic meaning. Each represents us. In the background of the Gospel we catch sight of a third "youth," the catechumen, who with the rite of Baptism takes off the old man and is reclothed with the new (cf. Rm 6:3–11; Eph 4:22–24; 1 Pt 2:1–3). The believer also has to be ready to follow the Lord at the cost of his or her life. That is why the catechumen was asked to remove his garment before descending into the baptismal bath. And after the baptism, the newly baptized received a white robe, symbol of the resurrection, and a lighted candle, sign of the new light that now illumined his or her life.

In this perspective we seek to travel through the Gospel of Mark toward the light. We ask ourselves first of all: Who "sees" in this Gospel? Who does not see? How does Jesus act with those who see—or believe they see—and with those who don't see? Do his words always bring light, or do they sometimes cause us to develop a certain blindness instead?

From Jordan to Bethsaida

*M*ark seems to weave a singular relationship be-tween the verbs "to come" and "to see," two verbs that connote the initial presentation of Jesus and that mark the whole Gospel account. The first time Mark speaks of "seeing" happens on the occasion of Jesus' baptism:

> As he was coming out of the water,
> he saw [*eiden*] the heavens torn apart
> and the Spirit descending upon him like a dove (Mk 1:10).

Grammatically the "seeing" here refers to Jesus, al-though he really experiences a vision. In this account Mark differs from the fourth Gospel, where the one who sees and gives witness is the Baptist (cf. Jn 1:32).

Jesus sees what remains hidden to everyone else. To his eyes the heavens open—even more, they are *rent*—and allow him to see beyond. He sees the truth about himself and about his relationship with God, who cannot be understood by anyone else.

Only Mark speaks of the heavens being "rent open" (*schizomenous*). At Jesus' death the veil of the sanctuary will be *rent* from top to bottom, so that even the centurion "will see beyond" and confess the Crucified's true identity (cf. Mk 15:38–39).

Jesus' glance

It is always Jesus who sees first. He passes, sees, and calls.

All vocational stories begin with Jesus, whose gaze focuses directly on the person and grasps what is unique and unrepeatable about him or her. First of all he grasps one's personal identity, well expressed by name: "He saw Simon and Simon's brother Andrew" (Mk 1:16). His seeing reaches the person in his or her uniqueness.

On the other hand, Jesus views a person's singularity within the family dynamic ("brother of," "son of"), in the concrete reality of daily life, and in the exercise of one's own trade ("while they were throwing their nets into the sea"; "at the tax collector's booth"). Work plays a big role in determining one's social identity. For the people in Capernaum, Simon is the fisherman and Levi is the tax collector. Jesus grasps all the aspects—both family and social—of one's personal identity. His glance goes from the center to the periphery, embracing the whole person from the most profound level, expressed by his or her name.

Jesus sees the heart and the feelings that live there (faith, for example), and, precisely because his look is capable of such depth, he can put the person back on his or her feet and make that person walk again: "Seeing their faith,

he said to the paralytic: 'My son, your sins are forgiven'"
(Mk 2:5).

But Jesus also knows how to see indifference and hostility, and in the face of these he adds: "Get up, pick up
your mat and walk" (Mk 2:9), provoking the wonder of
those present: "We have never seen anything like this!"
(Mk 2:12)

In certain situations Jesus' glance seems to follow a circular pattern, as if he wants to weave an imaginary circle or make a recon-
naissance (the verb that is used, *periblepô*, means "to look all
around"). One of these "looks" occurs in the house of Simon at
Capernaum. Someone tells the Master that his mother and his
brothers are "outside." In response, Jesus makes a turn of the room
with his eyes, looking attentively at all those seated around him,
and then adds: "Here are my mother and my brothers!" (Mk 3:34)

Jesus also "looks around" outside the house—for example, when he is searching among the crowd for the woman
who with much faith has touched the hem of his garment:
"But he kept looking around [*perieblepeto*] to see who had
done it" (Mk 5:32).

This "looking around" indicates Jesus' attention and
solidarity, as well as his ability to discern and weigh a situation. His look questions and provokes; it sees deeply,
beyond appearances.

The "look" of the scribes and Pharisees

The scribes and Pharisees can also "see," but their seeing involves something much different. For example, on

the occasion of Levi's call and the sumptuous banquet he gives to honor the Master, they say: "Why is he eating with tax collectors and sinners?" (Mk 2:16)

Their "seeing" stops at appearances. They look disdainfully upon transgressions of the Law. In Levi they see only "the publican." They don't see a sick person in need of healing; neither, obviously, do they succeed in seeing in Jesus the doctor and Savior of sinners. Rather, his "close association" with sinners scandalizes them. They recognize Jesus only as a transgressor of the Sabbath, a subverter of order and tradition. When they observe his disciples passing through wheat fields on a Sabbath, collecting and eating some of the ripe grain, they become indignant and cry out to Jesus to open his eyes and intervene: "Look [*ide*]! Why are they doing what is unlawful on the Sabbath?" (Mk 2:24).

They do not know how to see that "the Sabbath was made for man" (Mk 2:28). They don't know, or they don't want to see, that man is more important. Repeatedly "*they were watching* closely *to see* whether Jesus would heal on the Sabbath so they could make an accusation against him" (3:2). Their hearts are closed to mercy, and thus they provoke Jesus' indignant look: "He looked around at them with anger, saddened by the hardness of their hearts" (3:5).

The conclusion of this obstinate refusal to see is a fatal alliance of completely opposite ideological positions between the Pharisees and the Herodians, who join forces to eliminate their common adversary: "Then the Pharisees left and at once began to plot with the Herodians to do away with Jesus" (Mk 3:6).

"So that they look but do not see": the parables

Jesus is on the shore of Lake Galilee, where the people crowd around to listen to him.

> And such a large crowd gathered around him that he got into the boat on the sea and sat down, while the whole crowd gathered along the sea on the land. Then he taught them many things in parables (Mk 4:1–2).

In Jesus' public teaching, parables were his preferred method of addressing the people. In fact, at the conclusion of Mark's account of the parables we read that Jesus "spoke the word to them as they were able to understand it." Even more, "without parables he did not speak to them" (Mk 4:33). From these passages we might suppose that the parables were readily understandable. But if this were so, why did the disciples take Jesus aside and ask him to explain?

Mark 4:10–13 is a text that makes us question the parables' function. "To you," Jesus says to his disciples, "is given the secret of the Kingdom of God, but to those outside everything is given in parables, so that although they look, they may see yet not perceive, and though they listen, they may not yet understand, lest they turn back and receive forgiveness."

On one hand, Jesus seems to expect his parables to be understood. He is amazed that his disciples don't grasp this first one, which in some ways is a paradigm for under-standing the others: "You don't understand this parable? Then how will you understand *any* of the parables?" (Mk 4:13) On the other hand, the parable seems to have the purpose of blinding its listeners: "so that they look but do not see" (Isa 6:9–10).

This is a crucial text. Actually, a parable is effective when the one who hears it is able to see beyond the story, beyond the starting point of the narration (a seed, a jour-ney, a banquet, a business matter...). At first, the reference point remains completely hidden from the listeners. But when the parable "takes off" and its mechanism truly works, then one can see beyond it, grasping the parable's deeper meaning.

Intuition and decision come into play. Speaking about the Kingdom in parables, Jesus places himself, so to speak, on the threshold of seeing and non-seeing, and he dares his listeners to take the leap. Not by chance does Mark collect here the sayings of Jesus about the lamp—which is not to be put under a bushel basket or under the bed, but set on the lampstand (Mk 4:21)—and the invitation to pay attention, which literally resounds: "Consider what you hear" (*Blepete ti akouete*: Mk 4:24).

You have eyes and you do not see?

That Jesus' adversaries didn't know how or didn't want to see beyond is not very surprising. What is surprising is that the same thing is true on the part of his own townspeople and relatives. For Mark, Jesus' visit to Nazareth concludes with his tragic rejection, caused by the inability to see beyond what is in front of them: "'Isn't this the carpenter, the son of Mary, and the brother of James and Joses and Judas and Simon? Aren't his sisters right here among us?' And they rejected him" (Mk 6:3).

Such astonishment is almost embarrassing if one takes into account (and Mark doesn't do anything to modify his tone) that not even Jesus' disciples are capable of seeing beyond. Not even they succeed in "seeing" Jesus' messianic identity and the meaning of his mission.

After the second multiplication of loaves on the shore of the lake, Jesus decides to return to the other side. He therefore gets into a boat with his disciples, who, Mark notes, have forgotten to bring any bread along. And, as luck would have it, during the crossing Jesus talks about bread and warns them to "watch out for the leaven of the Pharisees and the leaven of Herod" (Mk 8:15).

The disciples interpret the event in light of the fact that they haven't brought any bread: "They kept arguing among themselves because they didn't have bread" (Mk 8:16). They don't understand Jesus' metaphor and can't see beyond the bag of bread! That this *misunderstanding* is considered grave is obvious from the series of questions asked by the Master: "Do you still neither see nor understand? Do you have hardened hearts? *Can you not see with your eyes? Can you not hear with your ears?*" (Mk 8:17–18)

With patience, Jesus reminds his disciples of the two multiplications of bread:

"Do you not remember when I broke the five loaves for the five thousand, how many baskets full of leftovers you picked up?" "Twelve," they said. "And the seven for the four thousand, how many large baskets full of leftovers did you pick up?" "Seven," they said. Then he said to them, "Do you not understand yet?" (Mk 8:19–21)

The disciples show that they have a good memory. They remember, but they don't know how to see what the facts themselves point to: Jesus' messianic identity.

Do you see anything?

In the Gospel of Mark, the sobering observation that the disciples *have eyes but do not see* is followed by the account of the blind man of Bethsaida (Mk 8:22–26), a healing which, because of the singular way in which it is done, suggests a symbolic reading. Mark recounts the story with a wealth of particulars.

First of all, Jesus takes the poor man's hand and leads him outside the village, apart from the others. Then the Master performs various actions, putting spittle in the man's eyes (it was believed that the saliva of a man of God contained a concentration of *spirit*) and placing his hands on the blind man. Next, like a good doctor, Jesus wants to know if the therapy worked, so he asks the man: "Do you see anything?"

The patient's response indicates an "already" and a "not yet": he has recovered some of his sight, but with a partial effect: "I see men, as if I am looking at trees walking around." It is striking that Jesus doesn't succeed in healing the man the first time around, but has to repeat the therapy: "Once again he laid hands on the man's eyes...." The new effect is surprising and is noted with insistence:

His vision was restored and he was able to see everything clearly (Mk 8:25).

Such emphasis seems intentional. Indeed, the healing of this blind man could be read as a paradigm for the account that follows; it is something of a hinge between the disciples' blindness and the proclamation of Peter.

Chapter Two

From Caesarea to Jericho

*T*he first part of Mark's Gospel has taken us through a dramatic alternation between vision and blindness; between the enthusiasm of the people, who say they *see* things they've never seen before, and the Pharisees' *refusal to see*; between the effort of Jesus' followers to *see beyond* and the obtuseness of the very same disciples. It has also shown us a Jesus who persists in his desire to cure a blind man both physically and spiritually. The cure of the blind man of Bethsaida establishes connections by contrast with the cure of the blind Bartimaeus, placed at the end of this central section dedicated to the following of Christ (Mk 8:27; 10:52).

Peter sees clearly, but...

The Master is on his way to Caesarea Philippi, and along the way (*en tê odô*) he asks his disciples: "Who do people say I am?" (Mk 8:27) Popular opinion reflects the final coming of Elijah, identified first with John the Baptist and then with Jesus himself (cf. 6:14–16; 8:27–28). Evidently the people see something. And it is true that Jesus is a great prophet. But this "seeing" is rather foggy, similar to that of the blind man after Jesus' first attempt to heal him: "I see men, as if I am looking at trees walking around" (Mk 8:24). Here, too, Jesus intervenes a second time, repeating the question: "But you...who do *you* say I am?" (Mk 8: 29)

And now, finally, someone sees very well, clearly and far: "You are the Messiah!" (Mk 8:30) Detaching himself from popular opinion, Peter recognizes in Jesus the definitive One sent from God, the Messiah. The narrative tension reaches a decisive point. By now, Jesus' identity has been revealed. At this point we would expect the transition to announcement: the good news can take its course (1:1). Isn't this what makes Mark the kerygmatic Gospel par excellence? Instead, we meet with a disconcerting silence—and not only that; we also encounter a stern expression on the face of Jesus: he "commanded them not to tell anyone about him" (8:30). The disciples were absolutely not to refer to what, through Peter, they had finally succeeded in seeing.

Why can't they announce yet that Jesus is the Messiah? Mark does not hesitate to explain. First it is necessary to follow the Master on the way of the cross and to lose one's life for the Gospel. Jesus begins to speak openly of his destiny and style as servant of the Lord. He will *have* to suffer much—not only death, but all that precedes it: rejection, hostility, scorn....

Peter's reaction is immediate; he takes the Master aside and reproves him. Perhaps Peter is afraid that his words will have a devastating effect on the others. In this context Mark describes another look of Jesus, who turns around and, *eyeing* his disciples, reprimands Peter. The disciples are under his gaze; it is he who has called them. Peter returns to his place: "Get behind me" (*Hypage opisô mou*).

In effect, Peter has tried overtaking Jesus. He has expected to stand in front of the Lord and tell him what is appropriate. Peter has acted as a generous man and a great friend, but without the discernment that comes from God. In fact, in trying to dissuade the Just One from his way, Peter has become a satanic instrument. He must therefore return to his place; he has to "get behind," because this was why he was called by the seashore ("Follow me": Mk 1:16–18). Then Jesus calls everyone together, disciples and followers, and without mincing words he enunciates the conditions for following him:

> "For whoever would save his life will lose it. And whoever loses his life for my sake and the sake of the good news will save it" (Mk 8:34–35).

Whoever wants to follow Jesus has to know that this is the way and there is no other. The term "Gospel" is used three times in the first chapter (Mk 1:1, 14, 15) and then not again, as if Mark sees the need of giving it an important introduction: the necessity to be ready to lose one's life in order to announce the Gospel. It's not enough just to see—not even for Peter. What is indispensable is to follow Jesus along the same road.

To see the Reign of God

Jesus next announces a "seeing" that will be condemnation for some and salvation for others. Whoever is ashamed of Jesus and his words, "Of him will the Son of Man also be ashamed when he comes in the glory of his Father" (Mk 8:38). Others instead will not die "until they see the Kingdom of God has come with power" (9:1). What does it mean "to see the Kingdom of God," and who are these fortunate people who will not die before they've seen it?

The narration continues with the account of the transfiguration: "Six days later Jesus took Peter and James and John along and led them up a high mountain" (Mk 9:2). Must we await the fulfillment of that promise? In effect, what takes place on the mountain, traditionally identified as Tabor, is among the most mysterious passages of the Gospel: Jesus "was transfigured" before Peter, James, and John. And they also "saw" Elijah and Moses talking with Jesus (9:4).

The story illustrates a tension between seeing and non-seeing. First of all, the three protagonists see "another" Jesus, a *metamorphosis* of their Master, in a glory that extends from his person to his clothes. This glory shines between Elijah and Moses, to such an extent that when these two figures disappear, Jesus' glory is no longer visible. It isn't possible to see the glory of the Messiah unless through the Scriptures, at the core of the Prophets and the Law. Peter, who has already confessed Jesus as the Messiah (Mk 8:29), curiously turns to him using the ancient name of Rabbi: "Rabbi, it is good for us to be here...." (Mk 8:5). Why precisely now that he sees the glory of the Messiah does Peter return to the customary title? Has he really seen who Jesus is, or is he still struggling to see?

The determining word comes from the cloud—symbol of the *Shekinah,* the presence of the Lord (cf. Ex 24:16; 34:5, 40:34)—at the very same moment in which the disciples are prevented from seeing. Elijah, Moses, and Jesus are enveloped in the shadow of the cloud (Mk 9:7) and are no longer visible, but from the cloud comes a voice testifying to what eyes cannot see: "This is my beloved Son, hear him!" And thus sight gives way to hearing. The disciples would have wanted to see more, but "as they *looked around,* they *no longer saw* anyone but Jesus alone with them" (9:8).

They go down the mountain together toward other visions, not of glory but of struggle and suffering (cf. Mk 9:14ff.). By now this is the reality to look at with new faith and courage. They are not to speak of what they have seen on the mountain, until the Son of Man has risen from the dead (9:9).

Contrasting ways of seeing

Coming down from the mountain, Jesus sees his disciples arguing with the scribes (Mk 9:14). A group has gathered around a father whose son is "possessed by a demon." The disciples have not succeeded in curing him.

Jesus asks that the young man be brought to him; he *wants to see him* up close. But the demon also *sees* and, in front of Jesus and everyone, gives vent to his complaints, throwing the boy into convulsions (9:20).

The scene creates a background for the personal dialogue Jesus has with the boy's father, a dialogue that starts off highlighting Jesus' interest—that is, his concern for the boy's pain ("How long has this been happening to him?")—and ends with the sorrowful plea of that father who wants to believe—that is, "to see beyond"—but who feels incapable of such vision: "I believe; help my unbelief" (Mk 9:24).

The father wants to believe, he wants to "see beyond," but nonetheless feels incapable of this kind of seeing. Jesus, *seeing* that a crowd is starting to gather and not wanting to make a scene, hurries to liberate the boy: "Deaf and dumb spirit, I command you, come out of him and may you go into him no more" (Mk 9:25).

Later on, it so happens that someone else begins to exorcise demons in the name of Jesus, with positive results. This does not escape the attentive and jealous eyes of the Apostle John, who immediately brings the situation to his Master's attention: "Teacher, we saw someone driving out demons in your name, and we tried to stop him, because he was not following us" (Mk 9:38). John is concerned with protecting the group's prestige and their potential loss of power. Not so Jesus, who sees the good, no matter where it's coming from, as part of his work (9:38–40).

There are other things, however, that Jesus sees with regret, among which are scandals caused to little ones (Mk 9:42ff.). In this context, Mark collects the sayings of Jesus about the worthless eye, or rather, the harmful eye that causes sin:

> "If your eye causes you to sin, pull it out.
> It is better for you to enter the Kingdom of God
> one-eyed, than to have two eyes
> and be thrown into Gehenna..." (Mk 9:47–48).

One thing that makes the Master indignant is his disciples' intolerance toward children (and probably toward their mothers who accompanied them). Seeing such intolerance, Jesus becomes angry and orders the disciples: "Let the children come to me. Do not prevent them. For of such as these is the Kingdom of God" (Mk 10:14). And he takes the children in his arms and blesses them.

Jesus, looking at him, loved him

Jesus is on his way to Jerusalem when a certain young man runs up to him, bows, and asks: "Good Teacher, what should I do to gain eternal life?" (Mk 10:17) Jesus reminds him of the commandments, and the man promptly responds that he has kept them all from his youth (10:20). At this point, Mark, unlike Matthew and Luke, leaves space in the passage for an intense gaze of love:

> As Jesus gazed upon him, he was moved with love for him (Mk 10:21).

Only Mark records this look. It's as if Jesus, before announcing such a radical request—"Go sell what you have and give to the poor"—wanted to instill confidence and courage in the rich young man standing before him.

Mark is also the only evangelist to specify that the face of the man darkened. He did not allow himself to be conquered by Jesus' glance, but went away sad (Mk 10:22; cf. Mt 19:22; Lk 18:23).

After the rich young man's departure, the evangelist again presents that typical "looking around" with which the Master captures his disciples' attention: "Jesus looked around and said to his disciples, 'How hard it will be for those who have wealth to enter the Kingdom of God!'" (Mk 10:23) And because the disciples are dismayed by these words, Jesus reassures them, profoundly fixing his gaze on them, as he did with the young man (the word *emblepsas* is used, the same verb form found in 10:21): What is impossible for men is possible with God (10:27).

That I may see!

Mark concludes this ample section dedicated to the theme of "following" with the account of the blind man of Jericho, offering a flexible model of what it means to follow Jesus. Only Mark names the protagonist and does so immediately, in Greek and in Aramaic: "Bartimaeus, the son of Timaeus," a particular point that argues in favor of the person's historicity. Mark describes the man with a certain thoroughness: he is blind, a beggar seated at the edge of the street.

Jesus is leaving Jericho and turning onto the road that goes up to Jerusalem. The blind Bartimaeus, questioning the passersby, finds out that it is Jesus the Nazarene who is approaching. There's nothing special in this information limited to a name and where he comes from, nothing particularly relevant for a Jew awaiting the Messiah. But our blind man processes the news and begins to shout: "Jesus, Son of David, have mercy on me!" (Mk 10:47) This is a remarkable declaration of faith. The title "Son of David" is practically a recognition of Jesus as the Messiah. Our Bartimeaus therefore sees what Peter has already had an inkling of: "You are the Messiah" (8:29).

Even more, Bartimaeus is aware of his poverty; in addition to faith, he requests help: "Jesus, have pity on me!" *Be for me what your name means: the Savior. Have mercy on me.*

Bartimaeus shouted loudly, and Jesus' followers "were telling him to be quiet." They are on their way to Jerusalem, and there is no time to lose. The Son of David has to inaugurate his Reign (the request of the sons of Zebedee took place in the passage immediately preceding). The disciples, therefore, rebuke the beggar and tell him to keep quiet, but he cries out all the louder: "Son of David, have pity on me!"

Jesus then stops and says: "Call him!" Bartimaeus does not lose a moment. Immediately, "he threw off his cloak, jumped up, and came to Jesus." He "threw off" his cloak! This is not a small thing for a poor beggar to do. That cloak represented a bit of everything, both abode and protection. It shielded him from the cold, but also from the humiliation of putting out his hand to passersby. It also guarded the little change and pieces of bread that were given to him out of charity. But as Bartimaeus feels himself called, he immediately throws aside his cloak. He does so spontaneously, as if liberating himself from anything that may be extra. What a contrast to the rich young man who went away sad, thinking of his riches! Here, without Jesus asking for it, Bartimaeus on his own throws aside the cloak and comes to him.

There they stand, finally, one in front of the other. "What do you want me to do for you?" "*Rabbi* [my Teacher], please let me see again" (literally: "to look on"). For Bartimaeus, Jesus really doesn't do anything unusual in working the miracle. He limits himself to saying that it has already happened: "Your faith has saved you." Bartimaeus has met all the required conditions. He has a faith that asks and that doesn't get discouraged when others wish to silence him; instead, "he cried out all the more." Besides leaving the little that he had, he spontaneously threw aside his cloak in order to run to Jesus. He therefore possesses the confidence that allows the disciple to follow the Master.

Jesus says to him, "Go," almost as if he wants to free Bartimaeus from indebtedness because of the gift he has received. But Bartimaeus, who by now sees things quite well, doesn't go. He has seen (understood) exactly where his good is and, full of joy, he follows Jesus along the road. It is the road that goes up to Jerusalem.

CHAPTER THREE

From Jerusalem to Galilee

Jesus' gaze in Jerusalem

Seated on a colt covered with cloaks (after Bartimaeus's example, others were ready to take theirs off...), Jesus enters the City of David to hosannas (Mk 11:1–11). He goes immediately to the Temple, but that day he does nothing but "look around." Mark reserves Jesus' "looking around" for moments of particular importance:

> When he entered Jerusalem he went to the Temple and, after *looking around at everything,* since it was by now the evening hour he went out to Bethany with the Twelve (Mk 11:11).

The following morning, as he heads for Jerusalem, his glance is drawn to a fig tree. Mark notes that Jesus is hungry and draws near to see if he will find something to eat; not finding anything, he leaves. Before doing so, however, he declares: "May no one eat fruit from you ever again" (Mk 11:14). The evangelist saves the fig tree's fate for the next day, the third on their way to Jerusalem. "As they were passing by early in the morning, they saw the fig tree shriveled up from its roots." Then Peter, not hiding his surprise, exclaims: "Rabbi, look! The fig tree you cursed has shrivelled up from its roots" (11:21).

In replying, Jesus recalls the importance of another way of "looking" at the situation; the disciples must learn to believe:

> "If you have faith in God, amen, I say to you, whoever says to this mountain, 'Be taken away and thrown into the sea!' and does not doubt in his heart but believes that what he says will happen, it will come to be for him" (Mk 11:23–24).

To the one who believes, "without doubting in your heart," everything will be given.

A free glance

While Jesus is teaching in the Temple, the Pharisees and Herodians arrive. Before asking the question to trap him—"Is it lawful to pay taxes to Caesar?"—they recognize in Jesus someone with an honest and independent look about him, that is, one who possesses a great freedom of judgment:

> "Teacher, we know that you are sincere,
> and show deference to no one;
> for you do not regard people with partiality,
> but teach the way of God in accordance with truth"
> (Mk 12:14, NRSV).

His adversaries therefore recognize Jesus as a person with a transparent gaze, free of favoritism and personal interests. He does not allow himself to be conditioned by "appearances" of a social, cultural, or economic nature, but truly sees in the manner of God: "Man looks at appearances, but the Lord looks at the heart" (1 Sam 16:7). It is this freedom of judgment that allows Jesus to observe well, even in matters of economics and social justice (cf. Mk 12:16–17).

Passing over other episodes, we pause at one that concludes the teaching of Jesus in the Temple. The Master is seated in front of the treasury and observes the behavior of the people:

> Then he took a seat opposite the offering box and watched the crowd toss money into the offering box. Many rich people tossed in a great deal, but when one poor widow came she tossed in two small coppers, that is, about a penny (Mk 12:41–43).

Witnessing this scene, Jesus' gaze speaks volumes. He sees something here and cannot remain silent about it; the truth of things, the strength of love. And so, calling the disciples to himself, he says to them: "Amen I say to you, this poor widow tossed in more than all the others who tossed money into the offering box—they all tossed in from their abundance; but she from her want tossed in all that she had, her whole livelihood" (Mk 12:43–44).

Once again the look of Jesus goes beyond appearances and sees the heart. From this perspective one can better understand the advice Jesus gave to his disciples immediately before this story: "Beware of the scribes.... They eat up the houses of widows..." (Mk 12:38–40).

Revelations and structure of scorn

The passion story illustrates a strong contrast between the "seeing" promised to the condemned thief and the scoffers beneath the cross. This tension first surfaces before the Sanhedrin. For a second time Jesus is interrogated by the high priest: "Are you the Messiah, the Son of the Blessed One?" (Mk 14:61) The secret that permeates Mark's entire account is exposed precisely now that the alleged Messiah is in chains. Jesus in fact breaks the silence about his identity and responds openly: "I am."

What are the grounds for this messianic claim? The only "evidence" Christ offers is tied to a future vision:

"...and you will see [*kai opsesthe*] the Son of Man seated at the right hand of Power and coming with the clouds of heaven" (Mk 14:62).

Two Scripture texts are cited—Psalm 110:1 and Daniel 7:13—both proclaiming the glory of the Son of Man. If at Caesarea Philippi Jesus begins to present himself as the Son of Man who must suffer (Mk 8:31), now this title affirms the glory that will come from suffering. The truth will be revealed, Jesus declares.

Mark's account gains momentum. The high priest cries blasphemy and tears his clothes. All who are present judge Jesus as deserving of death, and some begin to spit on him, mock him, and strike him (Mk 14:63–65).

Jesus is then paraded before Pilate, who points out to him an immediate need for "seeing"—one more realistic, given his claim to glory: "*Look* how many accusations they are bringing against you" (Mk 15:4). But Jesus does not answer him.

In the end, the "seeing" beneath the cross is composed of scorn. The priests and scribes ironically challenge the Nazarene to give miraculous proof of his messianic claim. "And you will see the Son of Man...." What of the promise of the Messiah and his assertions now? As a condition for believing, they want *to see him come down* from the cross.

> "Let the Messiah, the King of Israel, come down now from the cross so that we can see and believe!" (Mk 15:32)

> "Let us see if Elijah comes to take him down" (Mk 15:36).

They are the scoffers beneath the cross. In the end, whereas Elijah is not seen coming, the poor Christ can be seen dying.

The vision of faith

Finally someone's eyes are opened. Someone in the great darkness that covers the earth (cf. Mk 15:33) succeeds in truly seeing:

> When the centurion standing facing him *saw* that he had died in this way, he said, "Truly this man was the Son of God" (Mk 15:39).

God's greatest weakness—his not coming down from the cross, his death between two thieves, under the gaze of passersby who wag their heads and learned men who deride his promise—is the most bewildering and sublime occurrence, the arrival of the greatest love. That supreme hour is recorded by the feminine gaze:

There were also women there watching [*theôrousai*] from a distance, among them Mary Magdalene, and Mary mother of James the younger and Joses, Salome—they had followed him when he was in Galilee and served him—and many other women who had come up with him from Jerusalem (Mk 15:40–41).

Their gaze accompanies the beloved Master as long as possible, extending to his burial in the sepulcher:

Mary Magdalene and Mary mother of Joses *watched* where he was laid (v. 47).

These women had no other desire than to "see" him again as soon as possible and to anoint his body. So on the first day after the Sabbath, as the sun came up, they went to the sepulcher (Mk 16:1–2). They still remembered the large rock that had been placed in front of the sepulcher and were asking themselves who would roll it away, then behold:

...when *they looked up* they saw that the stone had been rolled away, for it was very large (Mk 16:4).

This first visual experience on the day after the Sabbath is already a source of trepidation. But inside the sepulcher the women experience a three-fold seeing:

When they went into the tomb *they saw* a young man seated on the right side, dressed in a white robe and they were astonished. "Don't be alarmed," he said, "you are looking for Jesus the Nazarene who was crucified; he is risen, he is not here; *look* at the place where they laid him! But go tell his disciples and Peter, 'He is going ahead of you to Galilee; *you will see* him there just as he told you'" (Mk 16:5–7).

One notes the progression of "sightings": from the young man, to the place where Jesus of Nazareth was entombed, to the Risen One. First of all, the women are protagonists of a direct and immediate seeing: they go in and *see*. They see a young man dressed in a white robe. In the second place, there is a seeing that is mediated by the young man. It is he who directs the women to accept the sign of the resurrection: *look at* the place where he was laid. And finally, there is a promised sight, the object of which is the Risen One: *you will see him.*

"He goes before you to Galilee. There you will see him."

The women, coming out from the sepulcher, "fled...for trembling and amazement had seized them." And, curiously, "they said nothing to anyone because they were afraid" (Mk 16:8).

So Mark's account closes. This rather abrupt ending, without any mention of resurrection appearances, must have caused problems even in ancient times. From here one can understand the addition of other conclusions: one was called "short" (placed between parentheses almost immediately after Mark 16:8 in the critical edition of Nestle–Aland, 27th edition); the other, called "longer," actually includes Mark 16:9–20. But perhaps our evangelist, who has surprised us throughout his account, intentionally finishes this way, with a type of "open ending" that entrusts the reader with the job of continuing the story. This is about a Gospel, about good news that challenges life.

The announcement to the women, "he goes ahead of you to Galilee," echoes the fulfillment of the word spoken on the night of the passion:

> "All of you will lose your faith because it is written, 'I will strike the shepherd and the sheep will be scattered,' but after I rise, I will go ahead of you into Galilee" (Mk 14:27–28).

The Risen One goes before his disciples to Galilee, as a shepherd who walks in front of his flock. In the Gospel of Mark there is a fascinating elusive quality about the Master; as noted earlier even when we think we have "reached" and understood him, Christ is always beyond us.

One has to return to Galilee—to the place where the preaching of the Gospel first occurred, to the country that first witnessed Jesus' proclamation of the Kingdom (Mk 1:14–15)—and to the ready and generous response of the first disciples (1:16–20). "There you will see him" (*opsesthe*). This same verb form is expressed in 14:62: "You will see [*opsesthe*] the Son of Man seated at the right hand of Power and coming with the clouds of heaven." Some exegetes interpret this as the eschatological coming of the Lord. The context, however, suggests the promised apparition in Galilee (cf. Mt 28:16–20).

None of this stops us from detecting in the passage an implicit ecclesial message: the disciples are invited to return to Galilee and risk another adventure. "Jesus of

Nazareth, the crucified, is risen, he is not here." Such an announcement signifies the real point: The account is finished, and the challenge of announcing it with one's life now begins. Mark, the Gospel of catechumens, proposes a journey in order to see beyond.

If the catechumen will have the courage to believe and to follow—if he or she will be disposed to follow the Son of Man on the way of the cross—then certainly that person will see him. Where and how? Not by way of external apparition; Mark, in fact, never mentions any. The believer will see the Risen Lord present in his or her own life and in the Church.

The Apostle Peter expresses a marvelous joy for those who love Jesus Christ "without having seen him" (1 Pt 1:8). This refers to second-generation Christians (and those who come after them). Thus, the beatitude pronounced by the Risen One is fulfilled: "Blessed are they who haven't seen yet have believed!" (Jn 20:29) In reality, this "not having seen and yet loving anyway" allows one to grasp the essential, what is invisible to the eyes but not to the heart: the truth of Christ and the fascination of following him.

"Come after me"

A Journey to Follow

CHAPTER ONE

A Cart with Four Wheels

rom the very beginning, Mark's Gospel presents a tight connection between Christology and discipleship. In fact, Jesus' encounters with people at the onset of his preaching in Galilee are realized through the invitation to follow him. Mark does not know how to see Jesus without disciples.

After John was arrested

Jesus leaves the desert and "returns" to Galilee as a kind of herald, "proclaiming the good news of God" (Mk 1:14). Previously he had left Nazareth in Galilee (v. 9) and gone to Judea, near the River Jordan, where John was baptizing (vv. 4–5). In solidarity with the sinful people, Jesus, too, went into the river and was baptized by John (vv. 9–11). After this he was moved by the Spirit and was drawn into the desert for forty days (vv. 12–13). Now news of John's imprisonment guides Jesus' steps toward Galilee. This succession of events brings us very quickly to the main point.

First of all, a new political-religious reality affects the scene: the delivery of John the Baptist into the hands of his adversaries. Jesus enters the picture when John is forced to leave it:

> After John was arrested, Jesus came to Galilee, proclaiming the good news of God (Mk 1:14).

The Baptist's dramatic end makes the hour strike for Jesus' preaching. In effect, Jesus is saying: *Now that the voice of the last prophet has been reduced to silence, my own will sound forth.* The measure of time is full: *peplērotai ho kairos.* The time of waiting gives way to fulfillment. Paradoxically, time reaches completion through the umpteenth setback of hope: through the murder of a just man and victim of arrogant power, through the prophet's martyrdom. Now the measure is full, and God sovereignly breaks into human history. Not in the form of a judge, however, but as Savior.

The good news that Jesus announces is the coming of God's Reign (*basileia tou Theou*). God's saving presence is so near that there is no longer time to waste. One must be converted now, immediately. One can and must change one's way of thinking: *metanoeite* (v. 15). It is necessary to convert and believe in the Gospel. We must entrust ourselves totally and unconditionally to the God who comes.

The first four

Mark 1:16–20 presents the call of the first four disciples, two pairs of brothers: Simon and Andrew, James and

John. These two vocational stories are told according to the same literary scheme. In main aspects they correspond perfectly, and in particulars they complement each other:

First Account: Mk 1:16–18

a) As Jesus PASSED along the Sea of Galilee,
he SAW Simon and his brother Andrew

> b) casting a *net* into the sea—
> for they were fishermen.

>> c) And Jesus SAID to them, "**Follow me**
>> and I will make you fish for people."

> bb) And *immediately* they left their *nets*

aa) and FOLLOWED him.

Second Account: Mk 1:19–20

a) As he WENT a little farther
he SAW James and his brother John,

> b) who were in the boat mending the nets.

>> c) *Immediately* he CALLED them.

> bb) and they left their father Zebedee
> in the boat with the hired men,

aa) and FOLLOWED him.

These two vocational accounts indicate some fundamental characteristics related to Jesus and the disciples.

Jesus is always described on the move: "and walking along the sea...," "and going a little farther...." He observes reality with a penetrating gaze. He immediately takes in the essential, an individual's uniqueness and profundity (one's personal name) as well as one's concrete existential history: family ties (brother, son) and social status (work). He takes the initiative and intervenes. His look becomes word: he calls to follow him. He promises a new identity: from fishers of fish to fishers of people. One notes that only the first account relates the Master's words; the second presumes them. How do the first disciples called respond? They have received Jesus' invitation in their everyday life—not on a Sabbath in the synagogue, but while carrying out their trade as fishermen. Their prompt response is impressive (*euthys,* "immediately") and is concretized first of all in *leaving* nets and boat (v. 18), their father Zebedee, and their partners (v. 20). The *leaving,* however, is not an end in itself; one leaves in order to "follow" (*akoluthein*), in order "to come after." The purpose of promptly leaving everything behind is the *following* of the Master.

The first four disciples follow behind Jesus without saying anything, trusting themselves to him totally.

More than Elijah and Elisha

This passage has a schematic, almost symbolic movement. More than telling us how things have gone historically, it indicates what attitudes characterized the first disciples who follow and what, according to Mark, must be our own.

A first level of investigation could come from a comparison with vocational accounts from the Old Testament. A paradigmatic passage for our text is 1 Kings 19:19–21.

We find here three key elements: an indication of the situation; the call (which in this case is effected through a symbolic action), and the following:

a) So [Elijah] set out from there, and found Elisha son of Shaphat...

    There were twelve yoke of oxen ahead of him...

        b) Elijah passed by him and threw his mantle over him.

            c) [Elisha] left the oxen, ran after Elijah, and said,

               "Let me kiss my father and my mother, and then I will *follow* you."

        bb) Then Elijah said to him, "Go back again; for what have I done to you?"

aa) [Elisha] returned from following him,

    took the yoke of oxen....

    Then he set out and *followed* Elijah.

The similarities of this account with Mark 1:16–20 strike one immediately. But in addition to the resemblance, certain significant differences are also noteworthy:

— Elijah calls in response to a charge from God; Jesus calls by his own authority and with extraordinary charismatic strength. Elijah doesn't say anything. He passes by, sees, throws his mantle, and continues to walk on. Jesus, instead, speaks and provides a reason for his call, adding a promise;

— Elisha declares himself ready to follow the prophet, but first he requests permission to say good-bye to his family. The prophet agrees. Not so in the two vocational stories told by Mark, where the response is immediate: *euthys,* "*immediately.*" This promptness underscores the arrival of end times, of the eschatological—therefore, one cannot lose oneself in secondary things. The response of Simon, Andrew, James, and John is immediate. They do not object. They do not even say a word. They simply leave everything and follow Jesus.

To leave in order to follow

Obviously we don't imagine Mark with a tape recorder in hand, running around from protagonist to protagonist and later reporting on what happened that day. His narrative outline is helpful in communicating a certain message on discipleship. The response of the first four called has exemplary value for us. It's as if Mark were saying: This is how one should respond! It is not so much the historical occurrence that should be emphasized, but the message that Mark intends for his community. Discipleship implies a radical response: to leave everything and to follow.

The first four called leave behind everything that was considered essential to make a name for themselves and to be successful. They leave their nets, their boat, their partners, and their father. It's interesting to note that the things they leave behind grow in a crescendo of importance: the instruments of work, nets and boat; the components of the fishing industry and the people who worked for them; and finally their father, the supreme figure within a patriarchal family.

Necessary things become secondary. The one, truly decisive thing is to follow Jesus. A little later on, Peter will say: "You see we have left everything and followed you" (Mk 10:28). Like Abraham, who left his own country, entrusting himself totally to the promise, so also Simon, Andrew, James, and John agree to leave their comfortable reality, trusting only in the word of Jesus.

And so, here are four men with the courage to follow him on his way, entrusting themselves and their future to the Gospel. Truly, the times are fulfilled and the Reign of God is brought near to Galilee!

Significantly, the paragraph that follows begins with an action verb in the plural: "and they entered Capernaum." Jesus is no longer alone; he is accompanied by four disciples who are ready to follow him.

Dialoguing with the Word

What does the following of Jesus involve? What kind of discipleship does Jesus ask for?

Three different elements emerge from the text:

a) Rabbis didn't seek out and choose disciples. Generally the disciple initiated things, presenting himself to the rabbi and demonstrating his desire to enter the rabbi's service, to become part of his circle of disciples.

b) Usually rabbis taught while seated, and the disciples formed a circle around them. (This memory was still vivid for Paul, who declared that he grew up in the understanding of the Scriptures at "the feet of Gamaliel.")

c) Rabbis effectively taught through explanation of the Scriptures.

Not so Jesus.

- It is he who takes the initiative in choosing. He goes personally in search of his disciples and calls them to follow him.

- Unlike other rabbis, Mark's Jesus does not instruct his disciples while sitting down and explaining the Scriptures. In the Gospel according to Matthew, the Master is seated on top of a mountain and the disciples are seated around him in a circle (cf. Mt 5:1); in Mark he is seldom seated (one exception is in the house of Peter: 3:31–35). Instead, Jesus is always moving, as though impelled by a certain urgency to encounter people, to heal the sick, and to preach the good news of the Kingdom....

- Those whom Jesus calls must follow him. That means that one becomes a disciple "going behind him" in the cities and the villages, wherever human history is played out. Formation is attained by observing what the Master does and by learning from his life, his way of being for others, and his way of acting. Jesus places no other conditions for following. If Simon and Andrew follow him, he will make them "fishers of people."

PAUSE IN PRAYER

Jesus also passes by today;
he passes close to you,

> as that day along the shores of the lake.
> He knows your NAME.
> He sees you as you really are,
> in the place where you are,
> in your affective and social surroundings.
> He sees you, he loves you, and he calls you.
> The most beautiful adventure begins
> when you feel yourself called by name
> and find the courage to walk behind him.
> You are not asked to leave for the sake of leaving,
> but in order to follow Jesus.
> There is a promise for you, too.
> Ask the Father, who sustains your response,
> that his Holy Spirit will give you the courage
> to follow Jesus,
> trusting yourself completely to his word.

Four wheels

Blessed James Alberione (1884–1971), the apostle of the means of social communication, spoke of the religious formation process by using the image of a cart with four wheels. Why a cart and not a car?

The image of a "cart" infers fatigue. This antique, rural image suggests that to go forward requires effort and guidance. The cart will not move by itself. You have to attach it to something that draws it forward. The formative process also requires some drawing on: one does not proceed along the road without wanting to walk it, without personal determination.

The four wheels must be stable and balanced if the cart is to go forward securely. If one wheel doesn't turn properly, the cart may move crookedly or even turn over. For Father Alberione, the "four wheels of formation" represented: piety, study, poverty, and apostolate. A spirituality that opens one to mission.

For a student of the Bible, the image of the cart evokes Elijah's chariot and the "cart of YHWH" (Ezek 1:4–28), the cart that transported the divine Presence, the *Shekinah*. Ezekiel saw it abandon the Temple on four wheels drawn by cherubim (chapters 10–11); it will return after the conversion of Israel (Ezek 43).

In Judaic spirituality (above all in the Kabala) and afterward in Christian spirituality, the image of the cart is read from a mystical viewpoint, with allusions to the glory of the Lord that comes to live within us. Along with the element of exertion, the cart-image reminds us that divine grace precedes our every determination to do good.

The evangelist Mark does not expressly use the image of the cart. However, he underlines the necessity of following, or rather walking behind, the Lord. It is a walking that should bring us to see his glory:

> "You will see the Son of Man seated at the right hand of Power and coming with the clouds of heaven" (Mk 14:62).

As Jesus stands before the High Priest and the Sanhedrin on the night of his passion, he quotes the prophet Daniel. The High Priest, an expert in Scripture, immediately understands the significance of this passage and indignantly tears his garments. We, instead, not as well versed in Scripture, need some explanation in order to get the full sense of the prophetic words Jesus uses. Until this moment Jesus has always spoken of himself as the Son of Man who must suffer (cf. Mk 8:31; 9:31; 10:33); now that his passion has begun, he speaks of the Son of Man "seated at the right hand of Power and coming on the clouds of heaven." For this glorious and apocalyptic vision, we return to Daniel 7:9–14, where the prophet, in his nighttime visions, sees a throne of "fiery flames, and its wheels were burning fire" (Dan 7:9). On this throne sits the Ancient of Days. The Son of Man, coming on the clouds of heaven, is presented before him, and from him receives power, glory, and dominion, a reign "that shall never be destroyed" (Dan 7:14).

While waiting to draw near to the throne with wheels of fire, let us do so in such a way that the four other "wheels" advance: faith and prayer, the proclamation of the message, and poverty. These are four dynamic attitudes that allow us to walk behind the Master.

CHAPTER TWO

Faith and Prayer

*M*ark does not hesitate to present Jesus at prayer. He speaks of the Lord praying when he recounts "the day at Capernaum" (Mk 1:21–34), a typical day that unfolds in the following manner:

In the morning, as usual on Saturday, Jesus goes to the synagogue where he teaches and amazes his listeners with the authority of his doctrine. This is the setting for his first miracle, an exorcism, and the consequent reaction of the people: "What is going on? A new teaching given on his own authority; he even gives orders to the unclean spirits, and they obey him!" (vv. 27–28)

Toward midday, he leaves the synagogue and is welcomed in the home of Simon and Andrew (this will be Jesus' home for as long as he is in Capernaum). Simon's mother-in-law lays in bed in the grip of a strong fever. Jesus goes over to her and heals her (vv. 29–31).

After sunset, at the end of the Sabbath rest, lo and behold everyone arrives bringing their own sick. Mark notes that "the whole city was gathered in front of the door"! Jesus takes care of the sick of Capernaum, heals many who are infirm, and performs other exorcisms. But he doesn't want publicity; he would "not allow the demons to speak" about him (vv. 32–34).

One can imagine that after such a busy day, Jesus would have enjoyed retiring for the night. But Mark does not mention this being the case; instead, he notes the following:

> Early in the morning, long before daylight, he got up, went off to a desert place, and there he prayed (Mk 1:35).

Before the sunrise

The Master *got up* at the first light of dawn, while Simon and the others were still sleeping. In this early rising is expressed that lively desire for God that characterizes biblical spirituality: "O God, you are my God, I seek you" (Ps 63:1); "...in the morning you hear my voice; *in the morning,* I plead my case to you" (Ps 5:3); "But I, O LORD, cry out to you; *in the morning* my prayer comes before you" (Ps 88:13). And again:

> It is good to give thanks to the LORD,
> to sing praises to your name, O Most High;
> to declare your steadfast love in the morning,
> and your faithfulness by night,
> to the music of the lute and the harp,
> to the melody of the lyre.
> For you, O LORD, have made me glad by your work;
> at the works of your hands I sing for joy (Ps 92:1–4).

For Jesus, it is not an obligation but a profound need to pray at sunrise. He desires to stay with the Father, to thank him, to listen to what he wishes, and to live in his love.

Mark specifies that Jesus "*went out* and retired to a deserted place." What does this "going out" mean? Couldn't Jesus have stayed in the house of his friends and prayed there? Undoubtedly, one can pray anywhere—outside or in, beneath a starry sky or in front of a spectacular sunrise, in the mountains or on the seashore, even on a street full of people and problems....

But in order to pray (wherever this happens) it is necessary to "go out" toward God. The action of Jesus, who leaves the house and retires to a deserted place is rich in symbolism and significance for disciples of all time. It's not a matter only of going out of oneself; going out to search and to find is required. It is a withdrawing, a standing apart that is directed at establishing an atmosphere of communion with the supreme "Other."

The verbs "to go out/to go in," while opposite, tend toward the same goal: to guarantee the *environment* conducive to prayer. One leaves in order to enter into communion. The Gospel of Matthew, in fact, speaks of "going in":

> "But when you pray, go into your storeroom and shut the door, pray to your Father who is hidden, and your Father who sees what is hidden will reward you" (Mt 6:6).

Dialoguing with the Word

How is your morning prayer
- The fulfillment of a habit?

- An expression of your thirst for God?
- Joy in dedicating the first moments of your day to him?
- A listening to the Word of God?

What difficulties do you encounter and how do you deal with them?

The desire and search for the Beloved is something that precedes the dawn, as was the case for Mary Magdalene, who went to the sepulcher "while it was still dark" (Jn 20:1). And the lover in the Song of Songs invites her beloved:

"...let us go out early to the vineyards,
and see whether the vines have budded,
whether the pomegranates are in bloom.
There I will give you my love" (Song 7:12).

Thomas of Celano writes of Saint Francis of Assisi:

He always sought a hidden place where he could adapt not only his soul but also his entire being to God. And if he felt himself visited by the Lord unexpectedly, lest he be without a cell he made a cell of his mantle. At times, when he did not have a mantle, he would cover his face with his sleeve so that he would not disclose the hidden manna (*Second Life of St. Francis*, chapter 94).

On the mountain in the evening

After the first multiplication of loaves, Jesus orders his disciples to get into the boat and precede him to the other side of the lake, while he disperses the crowd. Then Mark notes: "And after he took leave of them, he went up on the mountain to pray" (6:46).

Here too, as in Mark 1:35, the evangelist doesn't say anything about the content of Jesus' prayer. He limits himself to saying that it happened. Perhaps this is why we are even more curious. What did Jesus do by himself on that mountain? More importantly, what was his prayer?

Mark will wait for the moment of the agony, the dark hour in Gethsemane, to introduce us to Jesus' filial dialogue with his Father. Here he stops as if at a threshold and remains silent about the content of Jesus' prayer. But he makes sure we realize the great importance Jesus gives to it.

That particular day the Master had taught at length, right until sunset. Seeing that it was getting late, his disciples suggested that he send the crowd away. But he didn't want to do so, and instead ordered his disciples to provide for them: "You give them something to eat."

No matter how fast they moved, it must have taken quite a while for the five thousand to make themselves comfortable on the grass and to eat the bread and fish. It would have been quite late by the time Jesus sent away the crowd. After such a day, the weight of fatigue would have to be great. But, just the same, "he went up the mountain."

Could it be that Jesus would have taken the path up the mountain in order not to give in to sleep? In fact, "going up" always brings a certain exertion and requires that one stay awake. Toil and wakefulness are here oriented to the appointment with the Father, to prayer.

But there is something else to note. Jesus goes up the mountain to pray after a moment of great success, and in a probable mood of euphoria. John in fact notes that the people, enthused about what had happened, were organizing themselves to take him and make him king (Jn 6:15).

In this context, Jesus sends away his disciples and the crowd and goes up the mountain to pray. His strength does not come from the approval of the crowd or the admiration of his disciples. He draws strength above all from prayer and listening to the Father.

Dialoguing with the Word

- Do you stop to pray in positive moments, when you experience applause and success, or do you turn to God only when you have need of his help?

- Are you able to "send away the crowd" (i.e., thoughts, distractions, preoccupations...) in order to "go up" on the mountain and pray?

- What allows you or impedes you from "going up" and staying in prayer in your own concrete situation?

Prayer and liberation

When Jesus comes down from the Mount of the Transfiguration, he finds his disciples surrounded by many people and arguing with the scribes. The case they were arguing about involved a young man who was epileptic and was demonstrating all the strange reactions related to his sickness. It was normal for such a scene to attract a crowd (Mk 9:17–18). Mark, the Gospel of catechumens, lingers over the exorcism account, since it is worth speaking on the great theme of liberation from evil and demonic power. The enemy attacks us in many ways. In order to defeat him, our cunning and good will are simply not enough.

The text underlines first of all the disciples' inability to heal. Notwithstanding the power that Jesus had given to them when he sent them on mission (cf. Mk 6:7), none of them succeeds in liberating the young man. The father of the boy vents to Jesus: "I told your disciples to drive it [the demon] out but they couldn't" (Mk 9:19). The rest of the account underscores the contrast between faith and the power of Jesus. It is he who is the true protagonist. Around him are gathered:

- the people, in the role of "witnesses";
- the scribes and the disciples, to whom the failure pertains;
- the suffering boy to be healed;
- the father, who informs and supplicates Jesus;
- and finally, the demon, the great adversary.

How does Jesus behave? This poor father asks for compassion for his son and for himself. His prayer expresses hope: "If you can do anything..." a sensible plea, but he doesn't dare to ask more. Jesus encourages him but asks for a greater faith, reminding him that "all things are possible for the believer." Whoever has faith participates in the divine omnipotence, allowing God to act. Jesus helps one with uncertain faith to be able to pray. This man in fact revives his trust and at the same time clings to that of Jesus: "I believe! Help my unbelief!" Now Jesus can intervene with authority: "Deaf and dumb spirit, I command you, come out of him, and may you go into him no more." Then Jesus takes the boy by the hand and lifts him up. It is like a resurrection, a new life.

That miracle doesn't take away the disciples' bitter failure. Once they reach the house, they question the Master on their lack of success:

"Why could we not cast it out?"
He said to them,
"This kind cannot be driven out
by anything but prayer" (v. 29).

This conclusion allows one to glimpse a double reality: on one hand, the case in question was particularly difficult ("this kind of demon"); on the other, the early Church gave great importance to prayer in the performance of miracles and exorcisms. Only prayer is able to cast out certain obstinate demons.

Dialoguing with the Word

- The father asks Jesus to support him with his own great faith. The father's request includes implicit recognition of Jesus' perfect faith. We, too, can frequently repeat: "I believe! Help my unbelief!"

- In the passage we have just reflected on (Mk 9:22–24), prayer is connected with faith. What is this connection like in your own experience?

- Many people are overburdened with oppression, sadness, solitude. Intercede for someone close to you, asking with faith for that person's liberation from evil.

"Abba, Father!"

The setting is Gethsemane, where we find Jesus again in prayer. It is the night of betrayal and of passion. Jesus "took Peter and James and John along with him and he became very distressed and troubled, and he said to them, 'My soul is greatly distressed to the point of death; stay here and keep watch.' Then he went ahead a little, fell on the ground and prayed that, if it were possible, this moment might pass away from him..." (Mk 14:33–35).

While in 1:35 and 6:46, Mark wraps Jesus' prayer in silence, here he reports the Master's intimate dialogue with the Father:

He said,
"Abba, Father, all things are possible for you;
take this cup from me,
but, not what I wish,
but what you do" (Mk 14:36).

Jesus goes apart to pray, distancing himself first from his circle of disciples and then from his three most intimate friends. He is alone, kneeling on the ground and expressing his extreme sadness in the form of a prayer. Mark describes the scene as one in which the *suffering just one* raises his lament to God, laying his cause before him.

The phrase "he prayed" indicates a prolonged prayer. Jesus begs the Father that "this hour," the hour of suffering and death, would pass over him. His lament expresses the bitterness of one who feels his life threatened. There is the awareness of imminent abandonment into the hands of his enemies. There is the fear and tremor of death: "my soul is deeply grieved, even to death." Anguish, terror, grief to the point of feeling as if one is dying—the terrible anticipation of death in the depths of one's soul.

But his great sorrow and anguish do not override Jesus' full acceptance of what God, the beloved Father, wants of him. The Aramaic invocation "*Abba*," placed on Jesus' lips in this supreme hour of agony, expresses all the confidence, tenderness, and trust that he places in the Father above and beyond—and even in spite of—everything.

It is highly significant that Mark places this word on the Lord's lips precisely in his great hour of trial. If at this moment Jesus turns to God, calling him "*Abba*," it presupposes a great confidence developed through life. Jesus entrusts himself totally to his *Abba*, and even now he declares his unconditional obedience. "*Abba*" speaks of a filial experience that not even the agony of death can touch.

Jesus also teaches us to pray to God in this way: as Father. The early Church was very much aware of participating in the filial relationship of Jesus with the Father. The marvelous writings of Paul testify to this:

> You did not receive a spirit of slavery which caused you to be afraid; you received a spirit of adoption, by which we cry,

"Abba, Father!" The Spirit itself bears witness with our spirit that we are God's children (Rm 8:15–16).

And proof that you are his sons can be seen from the fact that God has sent the Spirit of his Son into our hearts, to cry *"Abba, Father!"* (Gal 4:6)

Watch and pray

After the prayer of Jesus, Mark addresses the theme of the disciples' sleeping with the exhortation to be watchful:

When he came back he found them sleeping,
and he said to Peter,
"Simon, are you sleeping?
Could you not stay awake for one hour?
Stay awake and pray that you will not come to the test,
for the spirit indeed is willing,
but the flesh is weak" (Mk 14:37–38).

The three disciples whom Jesus invited to keep watch are sleeping. Even Peter, who declared himself ready to die with Jesus (cf. Mk 14:27–31), is not able to remain awake. To him, therefore, the Lord turns directly: "Simon, are you sleeping?" The Master's question is full of bitterness: "Could you not *stay awake for one hour*?" *Not even you, Peter, who said you were ready to die for me!*

Before moving away from them again, Jesus repeats the invitation to keep watch and pray. The exhortation is addressed not only to Peter, but also to all the disciples. Why should the disciples stay awake and pray? For the sake of not falling into temptation. The temptation that threatens them is separation from Jesus: the "flight" that will take place at the arrival of his enemies (cf. Mk 14:50); the denial on Peter's part (Mk 14:66–72). Keeping watch and praying would enable the disciples to resist at the moment of trial. But they don't succeed in keeping watch:

When he came again he found them sleeping,
for their eyes were very heavy,
and they did not know what to answer him (Mk 14:40).

In contrast to the disciples' relapse, Jesus is again presented praying. He is the only one who is watchful and at prayer. And when everyone abandons him, he continues to entrust himself to the Father, right to the very end.

Vigilance and prayer are the conditions that allow us to confront the "weakness of the flesh." This weakness is the point of greatest fragility, that vulnerable part—our Achilles' heel!—through which evil temptation enters, leading us to sin.

Temptation, to which the disciples were exposed because of their faith in Jesus, can be overcome with prayer and vigilance. The disciples should in fact be ready to participate in the passion of Jesus, taking up their own cross (cf. Mk 8:34).

Dialoguing with the Word

The exhortation to be vigilant and to pray returns frequently in the writings of the early Church.

- What does "to keep watch and pray" involve for you?
- How do you handle trials and difficulties?

- In moments of pain, sadness, and discomfort, what is your attitude? Do you entrust yourself to God following the example of Jesus, who persevered in prayer?

CHAPTER THREE

Pay Attention to How You Hear

The evangelist Mark offers a twofold teaching of the Lord. The first takes place in the home of Peter, the second in a boat by the shore of the lake. The teaching Jesus imparts inside the house seems to make a distinction between those who are "outside" and those who are "inside," seated in a circle around him. These are the ones whom Jesus designates as his true family compared to those who are outside.

Brothers, sisters, and mother

This theme of the new family of Jesus is treated in Mark 3:31–35, at the end of a larger passage that began at 3:20 and reflects a technical composite that Mark seems to prefer: the so-called "sandwich structure":

A.	departure of the relatives:	**3:21**
B.	arrival of the scribes + the argument:	**3:22–30**
AA.	arrival of the relatives:	**3:31**

Mark 3:20 is situated in Capernaum, inside Peter's house, which had welcomed Jesus right from the beginning

of his ministry in Galilee (1:29). By this time, the Master had assembled a permanent group of twelve disciples to whom he gave the name "apostles" (3:13–19), and the house was subsequently open to hospitality, or rather taken by assault. A great crowd gathered, "to the point that they were not even able to get something to eat" (v. 20). This aroused suspicion and set in motion two opposing groups with a common purpose: to get to Jesus.

The prophet of Nazareth was gathering great success, and this alarmed both his relatives and the religious leaders. Jesus' relatives became aware of all that was happening in Capernaum and organized themselves to go after him. Worried about the political repercussions of such super-activity, they wanted to take hold of Jesus and bring him back to Nazareth. They considered him exhausted and out of his mind. "People were saying, *he's out of his mind*" (Mk 3:21)—an exalted son who had lost the sense of reality and needed to be kept under control in order to avoid ending up in the hands of the political and religious authority.

Actually, his fame had already reached Jerusalem, raising questions and preoccupations among "the experts in the Law." Certain scribes had decided to go to the place where he was teaching and, interestingly enough, they arrived sooner than his relatives (Mk 3:22). These scribes believed that Jesus was a pseudo-charismatic, a fraud who must have acquired his success through an alliance with Satan. Somewhat sarcastically they insinuate that his power to exorcise comes from Beelzebul, the prince of demons.

How does Jesus react? Mark presents him as being open to dialogue; he doesn't indignantly lock himself in the house, but accepts the confrontation, arguing and responding to their accusation. According to his habit, he speaks in parables. How can Satan cast himself out? If that were so, then his reign would be finished: "And if Satan rebels against himself and is divided, he cannot last, but comes to an end" (Mk 3:26).

At this point his relatives arrive, "his mother and his brothers" (v. 31). The text plays a bit with the outside/inside dimensions. His family sends someone to call Jesus *outside,* while Jesus recognizes as his family those who are *inside,* seated at his feet.

In the house of Peter

The fact that his relatives will not enter the house that welcomed Jesus is very striking. Why don't they go inside? Because of the crowd? Perhaps. The great influx of people, which Mark records at the beginning of the passage, prevents Jesus from eating and his family from coming in.

But there seems to be more going on than the fact of Jesus' great success. Through means of the house, Mark distinguishes those who are "outside" from those who are "inside." The house symbolizes the Church and plays a key role in understanding the extenuating circumstances underlying a teaching given "inside" as compared to that given "outside." To those outside, Jesus speaks in parables, but within the house he explains the mystery of the Reign of God (Mk 4:11). Let us go inside this house to observe what is happening:

A crowd was sitting around him (v. 32).

The scene depicts Jesus as a rabbi surrounded by his disciples. Mark is clear that many were present: a crowd was sitting around him (*ochlos*), gathered to listen to him. Within this context news arrives, and for the second time, from "outside":

"Your mother and brothers are *outside* asking for you" (v. 32b).

How does Jesus react? No invitation is issued to make room so that his relatives can come in. Here, as a matter of fact, hospitality is not in effect: this family visit is not one of courtesy. The Master's response comes in three parts: first in the form of a question, then with a look (v. 34a), and finally with a solemn declaration (vv. 34b–35).

In the first place, Jesus asks a surprising question, which sounds like he wants to distance himself: "Who are my mother and my brothers?" (v. 33) Then he responds with a long gaze: "And looking at those who sat around him…" (v. 34a). Only Mark makes note of this looking *around*, and he is insistent upon it. Twice he uses the preposition *perì*, "around" (as a prefix of the verb *peri-blepô*—"to look around"—and before the pronoun *peri auton*, "around him"). In addition to this, he specifies that those seated around Jesus were seated in "a circle." The Master is therefore at the center and his gaze travels in a circle. The group gathered around him is not an indifferent and chaotic multitude, but a circle of friends. They are many, but they all have a personal rapport with Jesus: they make up his new family. Before responding, he looks at them one by one, almost to verify the reality of their being there listening to him. Lastly, he adds the verbal response: "Here are my mother and my brothers." And he immediately explains the reason for this statement: "For whoever does the will of God is my brother and sister and mother" (v. 35).

Jesus begins his public life by announcing the Reign of God and inviting people to conversion. We have seen how the first four disciples left everything to follow him. Now he confirms his decision. He has already left Nazareth, but this is the moment for saying publicly: *I won't turn back! I will walk on the road that God has pointed out to me.* Before the crowd seated at his feet, Jesus confirms his own choice. He doesn't allow himself to be captured by relatives and taken back to be locked up, as he didn't allow himself to be captured by the scribes in a strict interpretation of official Judaism. He does first what he asks his own to do: the will of God (cf. Mk 14:36).

As we see in this passage, the *house* plays a highly symbolic role, creating a distinction between outside and inside. In the house of Peter is born the new family of Jesus, one not limited to the group of the Twelve, but made up of a multitude of people who do the will of God. The new family of Jesus consists of mothers, brothers, and sisters. In the early Church, Christians habitually called each other "brothers and sisters." The Father (of whom the text here does not speak) is for everyone the One in heaven.

Recent excavations have brought to light Peter's house in Capernaum. The area was transformed from the very first century by local faithful into a sacred place, and became the first and most venerated domestic church of Christianity. A modern circular room erected above it allows pilgrims to unite themselves ideally to the first community of disciples and believers.

Dialoguing with the Word

Imagine yourself at the Master's feet in the house of Peter:

- Do you want to be a brother, mother, or sister of Jesus? There is only one condition: "to do the will of God." The crowd "inside" the house recognizes in Jesus the One sent by God. The scribes and relatives of Jesus, on the contrary, would take him away from his ministry. This is how one opposes the will of God.

- Ask Jesus to teach you what is pleasing to God; ask him to help you learn abandonment to his will. The will of God is accomplished whenever one entrusts one's whole self to the Lord without reserve.

At the shore of the lake

As previously mentioned, the evangelist Mark always describes Jesus in motion and seldom seated. One of the few times this occurs, however, is in chapter 4, where the Master sits down in order to teach.

The scene takes place at the Lake of Galilee, near the outskirts of Capernaum. Jesus teaches from the boat while the crowd on the shore listens to him. Local Christian tradition places the preaching of the parables and the multiplication of the loaves at Tabgha, around three miles from Capernaum. There the land was, and still is to this day, uncultivated because of the rocky ground, although the area was rich in water (*Tabgha* is the Arabic translation of the Greek *Heptapegon,* or "seven springs"). Situated between the lake and the top of a hill, the place was able to accommodate thousands of people, something that would have been impossible in the narrow streets of the village or in the cultivated fields in close proximity to it.

After the so-called "private teaching" in Peter's house, Jesus commences with his public teaching in the form of parables (Mk 4:1–34). Here we are dealing with a chapter of particular importance for an understanding of Jesus' teaching, as well as an understanding of Mark's Gospel.

The evangelist's motives are diverse. Mark often presents Jesus preaching and teaching, but only here does he display the *content* of Jesus' teaching: the parables, told in the fourth chapter of Mark regarding the Reign of God. Right from the beginning of Jesus' public life, the "coming of the Reign of God" is presented as the central theme of his preaching (Mk 1:14–15), the horizon wherein his entire teaching develops. But what is this "coming Reign of God"? The argument will be elucidated in this recurring section of so-called "parables of the Kingdom."

He taught them in parables

The parabolic teaching is woven with tension and contrast. On one hand, it is presented as public teaching, imparted from the boat to a crowd seated by the lakeshore; a teaching particularly adapted to the people. On the other hand, it seems as if the parables have the purpose of making a distinction between the crowds and the disciples. The disciples, in fact, are given an understanding of "the mystery of the Reign of God" (v. 11a), but not "to those outside" (v. 11b), for whom the parables will have a disconcerting aim: "so that they will look but not see" (quoting Isa 6:9–10).

There is therefore a contrast between the didactic-pedagogic purpose of the parables and a purpose that we will call "blinding." How do these two aspects go together?

Even the relationship between Jesus and his disciples reveals a contrasting aspect. The apostles benefit from a separate, privileged teaching, which is Jesus' explanation of the parables (cf. vv. 10ff. and 34). And yet, notwithstanding his explanations, they don't get it. Their disconcerting incomprehension is all too evident.

How do these diverse aspects fit together in unity? This difficulty, fascinating and complex at the same time, has been the object of much study (among the best is that of V. Fusco). However, the parables still have a fundamental place in the teaching of Jesus. They represent his preferred way of speaking to the people: "He spoke the word to the people in many such parables, to the extent that they were able to understand" (Mk 4:33). At the same time, they constitute a veiled and provocative kind of teaching. They challenge and force one to think deeply and to take a position.

And so, we find ourselves ideally on the shore of the lake, listening to Jesus. The Master proposes to us three parables that speak of sowing.

The themes are developed in a certain symmetry. Only the parable of the sower is followed by an explanation, reserved to the disciples on the sidelines, and it is framed between two kinds of general affirmations. The resulting structure is therefore "concentric," with the parable's explanation of the sower precisely in the center:

A. Narrative introduction (vv. 1–2)
      B. Parable of the Sower (vv. 3–9)
            C. General statements (vv. 11–12)
                  D. Explanation (vv. 14–20)
            CC. General statements (vv. 21–25)
      BB. Parables of the grain and of the mustard seed
         (vv. 26–32)
AA. Narrative conclusion (vv. 33–34)

Paying close attention to the parable's language, we detect the presence of didactic terminology, with the verb *didaskô* ("to teach": Mk 4:1–2) used twice, and the word *didache* ("doctrine, teaching": 4:2b), appearing once. We also note the search for comparisons that illustrate the reality of the Kingdom. At verse 30, a twofold question highlights Jesus' effort to find appropriate comparisons:

"To what can I compare the Reign of God? With what parable can we describe it?"

We also find different invitations to listen:

"Listen now!" (v. 3)

"Whoever has ears to hear, let them hear!" (v. 9)

These invitations urge us to reflect and pay attention in order to understand. Jesus challenges our intellectual capacity. He exhorts us to apply the parable to ourselves and to stay attentive until what is heard with the ears transforms itself into authentic "listening."

Accepting his invitation, we pause over the shortest parable (Mk 4:26–29). This parable is not as simple as one might think at first glance especially since it could go by one of two titles: "The seed that grows by itself" or "The farmer who waits." Which title is more fitting? I opt for the second.

The farmer who waits

He also said,
"The kingdom of God
is as if someone
would scatter seed on the ground,
and would sleep and rise
night and day,
and the seed would sprout
and grow,
he does not know how.
The earth produces of itself,
first the stalk,
then the head,

    then the full grain in the head.
    But when the grain is ripe,
    at once he goes in with his sickle,
    because the harvest has come" (Mk 4:26–29).

The parable is introduced by a comparison ("as....like"): the Reign of God is like a man who sows seed. Three scenes or stages follow: the sowing, the growth, and the harvesting. The first and the third are quickly described; the stage of growth, however, is described in detail, almost in slow-motion.

a) *The sowing stage* (vv. 26b–27). What is the Reign of God? It is like a man (*anthropos*) who has sown seed. The conciseness of the Greek text succeeds in conveying the sense of passing time. Life goes on for the farmer—day and night, sleeping and waking; these extremes indicate the actions of a day. Meanwhile, however, the seed germinates and grows, without the farmer knowing how it all is happening. The earth bears fruit automatically (*automatê*), by itself.

b) *The growing stage* (v. 28). This stage occupies the central part of the parable and is developed in detail. The vegetative process is described step by step:

— the seed sprouts: the covering splits open and emits the germ;

— it breaks through the ground, growing and lengthening;

— the earth produces first the stalk, then the ear of grain, still empty,

— then the ear that is ripe, and finally the fruit, ready for harvest.

c) *The harvest stage* (v. 29). When the fruit has reached the *full measure* of awaited maturation, haste takes over. Immediately the farmer sends out workers, because the harvest has arrived.

Let's try to understand the point of comparison, that is, the parable's summit. What does Jesus want to call our attention to: the seed's fate, the farmer's behavior, or both?

If the point of comparison is the seed growing by itself, what does Jesus want to demonstrate? The unexplainable growth of the seed? There is undoubtedly something miraculous in the seed's growth. The earth gives fruit without visible cause and in a surprising way.

Instead, if the parable is about the farmer's behavior, what does Jesus intend to communicate to us? The farmer's patient and faithful waiting, or his swift intervention at the moment of harvest?

Here is an example of a parable with two "points" (like a mountain with two "peaks")! The entire account is meant to illustrate the Reign of God and the conditions for its coming. But the interpretive key is found in the parable's conclusion, where the images of the sickle and the harvest lead us to the theme of eschatological judgment. Allusion is made to a text from Joel:

Let the nations rouse themselves,
and come up to the valley of Jehoshaphat;
for there I will sit to judge

    all the neighboring nations.
    Put in the sickle,
    for the harvest is ripe (3:12–13).

The subject at the end of the parable is not the grain, but the farmer. It is on him that the story closes, and on his abrupt change from apparent inactivity to haste.

During the middle stage, that of growth, the farmer does not act. Whether the farmer is awake or asleep, nothing changes for the seed. The vegetation process develops on its own. Yet this does not mean that the farmer is not taking care of the seed. On the contrary, with expectant longing he awaits the moment in which he will be allowed to intervene. What else could he desire but harvest time? That was the reason he sowed the seed! The God revealed by Jesus shows himself as a farmer who respects the laws of growth; he waits during the time needed for the seed to germinate in its furrow and reach maturation.

The background of this parable hints at the problem of God's not intervening (harvesting). The audience to whom Jesus addressed himself might have had a difficult time conceding that the Reign of God was already in progress. They could have asked themselves the following questions: If God has truly decided to establish his Reign on the earth, why doesn't he do anything about it? Why doesn't he take the sickle and judge sinners now? Why does he allow evil-doers to peacefully enjoy life?

Jesus' response in the parable is that God awaits his hour without forcing it, as a farmer does not intervene before the grain is ripe. Our good God's nonintervention derives from his respect for the growth process; he waits until the seed has reached maturation.

Dialoguing with the Word

- Sometimes we may feel that God doesn't care about the growth of the word he has sown in us. But this is not the case. God has patience. He is like a farmer who awaits the maturation of the grain in the ear. What God has sown will ripen in its own time.

- Jesus exhorts us to have faith; in the in-between stage, the center stage of the story, the earth bears fruit by itself in a wonderful and inexplicable way. The essential is invisible to the eyes!

- In contemplation let us plumb the truth this parable reveals about Jesus' profound disposition. Unlike certain anxious people who would want God to intervene on their immediate orders, Jesus shows an absolute trust in the Father, who knows the right time for the harvest.

CHAPTER FOUR

Announcement and Poverty

*R*ight from the beginning, the disciples' call is oriented to mission: "Follow me, and I will make you fishers of men" (Mk 1:17). But we must wait until chapter 6 of Mark's Gospel to see precisely how Jesus associates his disciples with his own mission.

After Nazareth's failure

One day Jesus goes back to Nazareth, his hometown, in the company of his disciples. It's possible he hadn't returned there since his relatives had attempted to bring him back. At Nazareth there was a lot of talk about him. It was said that at Capernaum and at other places the carpenter's son worked miracles....

Now he is in the synagogue, this son about whom they know everything, having seen him grow up before their very eyes. There never seemed to be anything exceptional about him before, and they don't know how to make sense of things now:

> "Where did this fellow get all this?
> What sort of wisdom has been given to him
> that such mighty works should come about at his hands?
> Isn't this the carpenter, the son of Mary
> and the brother of James and Joses
> and Judas and Simon?" (Mk 6:2–3)

Nazareth does not allow itself to be "surprised" by Jesus; these people do not want to change their ideas. Their initial wonder ultimately gives way to incredulity and refusal. And so Jesus is forced to leave Nazareth, marveling in his turn at their unbelief. His own town does not accept him.

Mark records this rejection as something very serious. It is not merely an incident along the way, but a forewarning of what will happen in Jerusalem. The disciples are witnesses of it. The Master's defeats are in some way also their own. But they have decided to follow his destiny. There are other villages that are waiting:

> Then he went around the surrounding villages teaching.
> He summoned the Twelve
> and began to send them out two by two,
> and he gave them authority over the unclean spirits
> (Mk 6:6b–7).

The context suggests the idea of a certain "pastoral apprenticeship" of the disciples. Jesus is a wise teacher. Although aware of the urgency of the situation, he won't be rushed. First he calls the Twelve to live permanently with him. He wants them at his side to learn and to be witnesses, and to this end he involves them directly in his apostolic experiences. The different stages of their formative itinerary, from call to following to mission unfold in this manner:

1) he calls them to himself;
2) he sends them out two by two;
3) he gives them his own power of exorcism.

Let's pause here a moment on these three aspects.

The summons

Why does Jesus "call to himself" the Twelve? Are they not already close to him? Are they perhaps not following him? Does the *vocational call* not yet find a favorable response?

Mark does not tire in repeating that Jesus "called to himself": *proskaleitai.* This verb is particularly dear to him: he uses it nine times, while the evangelist John never does so. What does this verb say to Mark that is so important? It describes Jesus' initiative and gratuitous action. Remember when on the mount Jesus formed the group of the Twelve:

> Then he went up the mountain
> and called those he wanted [*proskaléitai*],
> and they came to him.
> He chose twelve,
> whom he also called apostles
> to stay with him
> and to send them out to preach
> and have power to drive out demons (Mk 3:13–15).

From a formal point of view, this "calling to himself" means naming the twelve out loud, so that those called can detach themselves from the crowd and gather around Jesus. In the Gospel of Mark, in fact, Jesus is usually surrounded by a large crowd that presses forward to see him up close, to touch him, and to present to him their sick with the request for him to heal them.

The Twelve are undoubtedly with him, but they are also part of this crowd, involved in managing the situation so it doesn't get out of hand. However, wanting to "call them to himself," Jesus has to say their names in a loud voice, articulating clearly. In this action of calling loudly there is present a kind of "subordination"; Jesus has an implicit power over those he has chosen. The mission is preceded by the *calling.*

Before sending the Twelve off on mission, Jesus *summons* them. He *calls them to himself,* as if to remind them that before going to others, they must strengthen their relationship with him. Let us, too, allow ourselves to be called again, perceiving again the attraction of Jesus' gaze and voice, the attraction of the One who calls us by name.

The mission

There is a particular method that characterizes the missionary procedure of the early Church, and Mark sees it as coming from Jesus himself: this going out two by two. Mission is an itinerant experience, but not one that is done alone.

Why does Jesus send his "missionaries" in pairs? The text doesn't say, but the context suggests a reason. Going out to others must witness to a love for one another. It has to be realized "together," first accepting in the brother or sister missionary walking at your side the saving presence of the Lord in whose name both are sent. This witness to charity simultaneously becomes a witness to truth: the beautiful news is attested jointly by the two witnesses. The method is not unimportant. Mission must witness to the mutual love that unites those who are sent with those to whom they are sent.

There emerges a mission that is accomplished *together*, overcoming the temptations of individualism and of acting on one's own. Jesus does not send us alone, but with others—therefore, jointly responsible for the mission and for the missionaries.

With the power to liberate

To the Twelve who are sent, Jesus confers his power over demons; the power of exorcism, of *liberation*. Where the salvific Reign of God is announced, satanic power in all its expressions is cast out.

The announcement of salvation goes hand in hand with the coming liberation. The early Church was well aware of this. This power of liberation comes directly from Jesus and is conferred precisely in view of mission: "he gave them authority over the unclean spirits" (Mk 6:7). We are dealing here with the liberation and healing of various kinds of sicknesses stemming from both psychic and social oppression, as well as from the oppression of religious formality (cf. 7:14–23).

In the Gospel of Mark, Jesus' first miracle is precisely the healing of the possessed man, the exorcism of an "unclean spirit" (Mk 1:23–27). The miracle, which takes place in the synagogue of Capernaum, confirms the authority of Jesus' teaching. And the people enthusiastically exclaim: "What's going on? A new teaching given on his own authority; he gives orders to the unclean spirits, and they obey him!" (1:27)

The disciples are sent to evangelize, but in the manner of their rabbi: by liberating from oppression.

Dialoguing with the Word

- The Lord also sends you, as he did his first disciples. The Christian life, in fact, is by its very nature a going forth to others in the name of Jesus and with the liberating power of his Gospel. How do you live the missionary dimension of your faith?

- Jesus calls to himself; he sends the disciples out two by two; he confers on them his power of liberation. Do you live mission as a gift? Do you allow yourself to be attracted by Jesus? Do you commit yourself to collaborating with others, or do you work alone, accountable to no one?

- In the language of Mark, going "two by two" means to allow oneself to be helped reciprocally by a brother, by a sister. Are you convinced that love

> among ourselves, in the community of the Church, is
> the most effective form of evangelization? Do you
> commit yourself in this sense? Do you believe in the
> power of liberation that has been given to you? What
> can you do, in your concrete situation, to make
> Christ's power to liberate others efficacious?

The poverty of those sent

Those who are sent receive instructions regarding their clothes and the way to behave. They must distinguish themselves with a radical poverty, which however is not an end in itself, but a sign of extreme trust in him who sends them and protects them.

> He summoned the Twelve
> and began to send them out two by two,
> and he gave them authority over the unclean spirits
> and ordered them to take nothing on the road
> except a staff—
> not bread,
> not a bag,
> nor money in their belts—
> but instead to put sandals on their feet
> and not to wear two tunics (Mk 6:7–9).

The first part of the account is an instruction on what the missionary can bring along. Only pure essentials: a walking stick, sandals, a tunic. Replacements are prohibited (another pair of sandals, a second tunic). It is forbidden to guarantee oneself a margin of security: neither bread nor money. It is forbidden, moreover, even to have what the poor are careful to have: a knapsack to carry bread and the goods received in alms.

What is Mark trying to say here? Why does he consider the first missionaries' manner of dressing and behaving worthy of handing on?

First of all, it should be noted that these instructions are introduced as a command from Jesus: "he ordered them" (*parangéllein*). In the Church everything regarding mission can be traced back to Jesus, even the rules of dress.

In the second place, we notice that these instructions are addressed to itinerant missionaries. We could title them: "Advice for the trip." The Twelve are to be sent in pairs, according to the plan already presented in their call (cf. Mk 1:16–20; 3:13–19). These instructions are continued in the early Church: the Book of Acts refers to the sending of Paul and Barnabas, of Peter and John.

The exhortation to not take anything with oneself, neither clothing nor provisions (bread) nor money, can be read in conjunction with Mark 10:28, that is, as a total renunciation of every possession. Even more, it can be seen as a renunciation of every need. Someone has seen here a similarity with the practices of the cynic-stoic philosophers, who wandered around with a walking stick (itinerancy), a mendicant knapsack, and a philosopher's mantle. But the expression "no bread" sounds even more radical than the proverbial austerity of the cynics, whose diet provided for "a little bit of bread accompanied by figs and water to drink" (Philemon in *Diog. Laert.* 7:27).

It is good to see other differences between the Marcan text and the customs of the Greek philosophers. Let's take for example the knapsack: the cynics' clothing symbolically represented a point of contact with the image of the mendicant, being a mendicant philosopher of wisdom and truth. For Mark, instead, Christian missionaries should not carry knapsacks. Therefore there is a different outlook behind their poor dress.

In fact, the portrait of the itinerant missionary, seen up close, moves away from that of the mendicant philosopher. What is behind the missionaries' radical poverty? Unconditional trust in the One who sends them.

Those who are sent must learn to entrust themselves to daily Providence without "storing up" for tomorrow, like Israel in the desert, which had to gather a sufficient measure of manna every day. Anything beyond what was necessary, taken out of greed or anxiety for tomorrow, was destined to putrefy (cf. Ex 16:16–20).

The Twelve are sent by Jesus to the dispersed house of Israel, with nothing else but the pilgrim's indispensable raiment: sandals, tunic, and walking stick. They are not to carry a knapsack, because he who sends them provides for their daily bread and for everything else they will need.

The work they are sent to do is not their own, it belongs to another. God himself is involved in the missionary activity of Jesus and his disciples. They must not take a knapsack, because their knapsack is God.

Dialoguing with the Word

Deepen in contemplation the poverty-trust relationship that emerges in Mark 6:7–9:

- How do you live the value of Christian poverty?

- Have you ever experienced the privation of something that seemed necessary?

- Ask Jesus, the Poor One of the Lord, for the grace to entrust yourself to his word without excessive worry for your future.

Jesus recommends to the Twelve a style of mission that faithfully follows his own behavior. He asks his disciples—and he asks us—to share not only the exterior aspect of his behavior (poverty of life and of means), but above all the motivations that sustain it. He is the Poor One who has no need of a knapsack. He knows how to draw from the Father's inexhaustible richness.

- Can you say that the soul of your "poverty" is trust?

- Ask Jesus for his unconditional trust in the Father.

CHAPTER FIVE

The Heart of a Shepherd

While the disciples are on mission, Mark recounts that Jesus' renown reaches Herod's court and is immediately linked to the death of John the Baptist:

...People were saying,
"John the Baptizer has been raised from the dead,
and that is why these powers are at work in him"
[i.e., the power of miracles].
But others said, "It is Elijah."
And others said,
"It is a prophet like one of the prophets of old."
But when Herod heard it, he said,
"John, whom I beheaded,
has been raised" (Mk 6:14–16).

With this "intermission" dealing with the fame of Jesus and the Baptist's death, Mark offers proof of the lively eschatological expectation that existed in his contemporaries. They lived in fervent anticipation of the Messiah. Jesus, like John before him, is identified as Elijah, the prophet who would return at the end times, right before the Messiah.

Then the Twelve return, full of enthusiasm. They are longing to tell Jesus of their first missionary experience:

Then the apostles gathered around Jesus
and told him all that they had done
and had taught (Mk 6:30).

Jesus takes care of his disciples

We can picture the scene. Jesus is awaiting his disciples' return with a certain trepidation. The bottom line is that this has been their first experience "on their own," without him. Now they return, and he gathers them around himself like a hen with her chicks, like a shepherd with his sheep: "they gathered around Jesus." They tell him everything that they have *done* (they were sent, in fact, to work, to expel demons) and all that they have *taught*. Their desire to recount everything is great and the time is short, because the crowd continues to press around them:

There were so many people coming and going
that they didn't even have time to eat.
And he said to them,
"Come away privately, just yourselves,
to a desert place
and rest for a bit" (Mk 6:32, 31).

This splendid brushstroke of Mark illustrates with affectionate strength the care the Good Shepherd has for his apostles. They leave together in a boat, toward a place set apart. Our gaze follows them as they leave.

Jesus actually reveals himself as Master and Shepherd. From him came the initiative for mission; from him comes the initiative for refreshment, for a kind of reflective break in peace and quiet. He "convenes" his disciples both before and after their mission, not to ask them an account but to reinforce the bonds of affection and friendship. Jesus offers the apostles the support and welcome they need, and, above all, his intimacy.

Dialoguing with the Word

In the boat taking the disciples to a place apart we can recognize the Church and realize that Jesus offers us, too, the possibility of staying with him and of telling him all that we have done. The apostolic dimension of our life takes on strength and perseverance from the care that he provides for us. The Good Shepherd offers us time to stay with him and to tell him of our experiences.

- How do you live your "return" from mission, that is, the moments following an apostolic experience or encounter?

- Do you speak with Jesus about the successes and difficulties that you've encountered?

- Do you allow yourself to be confronted with the Word and the community, or do you process things on your own?

He was moved to compassion

Jesus and his disciples disembark from the boat that took off from shore in search of a solitary place, where they could rest somewhat and be together.

And here, instead, something unforeseen happens. Someone had observed them, guessed their plans, and started after them. Others followed. The desire to listen to Jesus was so strong that the whole crowd directed itself toward the place Jesus had chosen for a time of rest. By the time the boat arrives, the crowd is already there.

> ...People saw them leaving
> and many of them found out where he was going
> and they ran ahead on foot from all the towns
> and got there before them.
> When he got out of the boat
> he saw a large crowd,
> and he was moved with pity for them
> because they were like sheep without a shepherd,
> and he began to teach them many things
> (Mk 6:33–34).

Seeing that great multitude, Jesus is moved to profound compassion. These people, who have walked beneath the heat of the sun to listen to his word, make him forget, in a certain sense, the reason he and the disciples had left in the first place. How could he rest, ignoring their need, their hunger and thirst for truth? In his imagination springs the picture of the sheepfold, an image beloved in Scripture. But the image falls short of the idyllic scriptural icon. The people before him are a dispersed flock, sheep abandoned for lack of a shepherd. They seek food, meaning, and direction in life.

> *Kai esplanchnisthê ep'autous.*
> He was moved with pity for them (Mk 6:34).

He had retired to give time and a special reception to his disciples, but this multitude touches his heart. Matthew, in the parallel passage, adds: "they were worried and helpless" (Mt 9:36). Faced with humanity left to its own devices, Jesus incarnates divine compassion.

Mark does not describe any external signs of Jesus' compassion, but the Greek verb he uses expresses a very strong reality. The word *splanchna* means the bowels, in particular the maternal womb. He therefore indicates a "visceral" compassion that grasps Jesus completely.

In Mark, the verb *splanchnizomai* describes Jesus' compassion for suffering humanity. It occurs first of all in the context of the leper's healing, that is, before a man forced to cry out his humiliating and pitiful situation so that others, those who are healthy, would keep their distance. Yet this leper breaks the law and approaches Jesus: "If you wish to, you can make me clean!" (Mk 1:40) Then Jesus "was moved with compassion"; he stretches out his hand and, in his turn transgressing Judaic norms, touches the leper and says to him: "I do wish it, be made clean" (v. 41).

The verb *splanchnizomai*—"to have compassion"—reappears next in the multiplication of the loaves, in Mark 8:2. Jesus' compassion for the multitudes is the source from which his apostolic activity springs.

We could say that *splanchnizomai* translates as a typical divine expression and not a simple human emotion. It indicates the compassion of God toward his people and characterizes the messiahship of Jesus. In Matthew and

Luke this verb also reveals Jesus' way of being and acting. Three parables attest to this:

• Mt 18:23–25: the owner who, "moved to compassion," forgave his servant his debt, while the servant, in the face of his own indebtedness to others, acted without mercy.

• Lk 10:29–37: the Good Samaritan, who drew near to the Jew beaten by robbers and was the only one who stopped to give him help.... The rivalry that existed between Jews and Samaritans made this Samaritan's sentiments stand out all the more: "when he saw him he took pity" (v. 33).

• Lk 15:11–32: the forgiving father who accepted his returning prodigal son: "his father saw him and took pity and he ran and fell upon his neck and kissed him repeatedly" (v. 20). The Old Testament story that forms a backdrop for this scene is that of David, who burst into tears when told of the death of the son who had attempted to take his throne. David is shaken at the news of his death: "O my son Absalom, my son, my son Absalom! Would I had died instead of you, O Absalom, my son, my son!" (2 Sam 18:33). Here David rises above himself, so to speak. He exemplifies the sentiments of God.

And so it is in the parables of Jesus. God is like the owner who, moved to compassion, forgives the entire debt; he is like the Samaritan who, moved to compassion, bends down to the man beaten by the robbers; he is like the father who never tires of welcoming his wayward son.

Jesus incarnates this immense divine compassion. He expresses the *pathos* of God toward his people, a profound and incomprehensible *pathos.*

What does this compassion provoke in Jesus? What is his response? The text reads: "*êrxato didaskein,*" "he began to teach" (Mk 6:34). This response is characteristic of Mark. In fact, in the parallel passage, Matthew underscores Jesus' therapeutic activity: "When he got out of the boat he saw a large crowd, and he was moved with pity for them and healed their sick" (Mt 14:14). Mark, instead, presents Jesus as the Good Shepherd, who reunites the flock through his *teaching.* He feeds the sheep above all with the bread of the Word.

Word and bread

The people have gathered to listen to the Master. Jesus doesn't seem to be aware of the passing of time. So the disciples intervene:

> "This is a desert place and it is already late;
> send them away
> so they can go off to the farms and villages
> and buy themselves something to eat" (Mk 6:35–36).

Jesus, however, does not intend to dismiss the crowd in this way: "*You* give them something to eat." The disciples do not understand that the Master is associating them with his pastoral ministry: "Should we go buy two hundred denarii worth of bread and give it to them to eat?" (6:37)

First of all, they will have to tally up what provisions already exist among the people, what means they have available: "How many loaves do you have? *Go see.*" An investigation leads to the response: "Five loaves and two fish."

The rest of the account sheds light on this passage's surprising connection with Psalm 23. Jesus has the people sit down on the green grass (only Mark mentions this particular point, which recalls Ps 23:2) in groups of hundreds and fifties. He reestablishes in this way a fraternal situation, presupposed for the banquet. These groups seated in a circular pattern on the green grass resemble *flower beds.* Mark actually uses the words "flower bed" to indicate the "groups." Perhaps the different-colored clothing suggested this image to him. Or, more likely, there is some link with Jewish tradition. There is a rabbinic saying that has the same image of the "flower bed":

"When the disciples sit down like so many flower beds
and they are busy with the Torah,
I will come down close to them"
(Strack-Billerbeck, II, 13).

The scene is undoubtedly striking. These groups/flower beds of hundreds and fifties seated on the green grass, having fed themselves with the Word, now fraternally share bread and other food.

Jesus is the new Moses, *the eschatological shepherd.*

In the desert Moses shepherded Israel with the Word of God and fed them with manna and quail, bread and meat from heaven. In an analogous way, Jesus, in this solitary desert place, first of all gathers the flock around the banquet of the Word. Now the sheep are on the green grass (at the Messiah's arrival the desert will bloom!), around their shepherd. And Jesus, as the new Moses, multiplies the bread. The reference to manna is evident. One could probably also speak of a connection between the fish and the quail. In the account from Genesis, in fact, birds and fish are both created on the fifth day (Gen 1:20–23).

What matters more is the image that Mark gives here of Jesus: he is more than a prophet, he is the *Shepherd of Israel.* His pastoral mission gushes forth from the heart of God, from *compassion* for the people.

The apostles are associated with Jesus' pastoral ministry, involved firsthand as his assistants. Their duty recalls the work that Moses entrusted to the elders (cf. Ex 18:21–25).

After pronouncing the blessing and breaking the bread, Jesus "kept giving them to the disciples to distribute to the people" (Mk 6:41). With this gesture the apostles are given rule of the people of God and the duty to "give them something to eat." This expression is clearly allusive of their pastoral ministry. The disciples are invited to distribute the riches of the Lord's banquet in order that all will have enough to eat and will rejoice in the benevolent love of which the psalm speaks: "goodness and mercy shall follow me all the days of my life" (Ps 23:6).

Dialoguing with the Word

Stop to contemplate Jesus' compassion for the crowd. Ask Jesus to let you participate in his charity. Make this your prayer:

Jesus, Good Shepherd,
who brought from heaven the fire of your love,
give us your heart.
Inflame us with desire for the glory of God
and with a great love for our brothers and sisters.
Make us sharers in your apostolate.
Live in us, that we may radiate you
in word, in suffering,
in pastoral action,
in the example of a good life.
Dispose all minds and hearts to receive your grace.
Come, divine Shepherd, guide us;
may there soon be one flock and one Shepherd. Amen.

(Blessed James Alberione)

CHAPTER SIX

If Anyone Wants to Follow Me

*T*aking off from Peter's confession, Mark dedicates a long section to the theme of following Jesus. Characteristic of this section are three announcements of the passion, punctually followed by the incomprehension of Peter and the disciples:

Announcement of the passion		Incomprehension	
8:31	1st announcement	8:32–33	incomprehension of Peter
9:30–31	2nd announcement	9:32	incomprehension of the disciples
10:32–34	3rd announcement	10:35–40	incomprehension of the two sons of Zebedee

Jesus announces the entire paschal mystery: his suffering, humiliation, and death, but also the resurrection. Nevertheless, he's not understood. The way of the cross is not in tune with his disciples' messianic conception.

The first to actually rebel is Peter, who tries to make the Master fit inside his own messianic vision, dissuading him from the road of the passion: "he began to rebuke him" (*erxato epitimân autô*: Mk 8:32). In his turn, however, Jesus "reproves" Peter (using the same verb!) and orders him to stay in his place: "behind" and not *in front*. Jesus calls him *Satanâ*, because he is taking the part of the tempter rather than of the friend who seeks the will of God. Then the Master calls the crowd and his disciples and, without mincing words, declares to everyone the conditions for following him:

> "If anyone would be my disciple,
> he must deny himself
> and take up his cross
> and follow me" (Mk 8:34).

The first thing that is evident here is that Jesus proposes, he does not impose. He appeals to our liberty: "If anyone wants..." No one is obliged to follow him. But if someone wants to, then that person must remember two fundamental conditions: denying oneself and taking up one's own cross.

What does it mean *to deny yourself*? We could interpret it as renouncing one's self-realization, giving up one's own instincts and vital interests. It is the kind of renouncing that has as its counterpart total trust in the One who gives and guarantees life: the God of Jesus Christ.

Taking up your own cross speaks of complete trust. When Mark writes his Gospel, this expression already has a certain connotation; in the Christian community it is inseparable from the martyrdom of Jesus and includes also willingness on the part of his followers to be martyred. But when Jesus pronounced this word, perhaps he was not thinking of the scaffold of the cross. In fact, although he announces that he must suffer much, that he will be rejected by the elders, the high priests, and the scribes, and that he will be put to death (Mk 8:31), he doesn't say how. He never says: "I will be crucified."

So what then does this expression mean in the mouth of Jesus, this "taking up your own cross"? Some have interpreted it in continuity with Ezekiel 9, understanding in the term *stauros*—"cross"—the *Tau* symbol: the sign of entrusting oneself to the Lord. It's helpful to bear in mind the following prophetic background:

> Then he cried in my hearing with a loud voice, saying, "Draw near, you executioners of the city, each with his destroying weapon in his hand." And six men came from the direction of the upper gate, which faces north, each with his weapon for slaughter in his hand; among them was a man clothed in linen, with a writing case at his side. They went in and stood beside the bronze altar.
>
> Now the glory of the God of Israel had gone up from the cherub on which it rested to the threshold of the house. The LORD called to the man clothed in the linen, who had the writing case at his side and said to him, "Go through the city, through Jerusalem, and put a mark on the foreheads of those who sigh and groan over all the abominations that are committed in it" (Ezek 9:1–4).

In Ezekiel's prophetic vision, the sign of the Tau, a T on the forehead of those who sigh and lament over the iniquities and injustices committed in Jerusalem, comes to mean that God signs those whom he separates from the

perverse logic of the world and who entrust themselves to
him. To take up your own cross is equivalent in this sense
to being signed by the Lord, to whom we entrust ourselves
completely.

Mark therefore gathers a series of four sayings using
the particle *gar* ("for"). These illustrate the necessity of
giving up everything, even one's own life, for the cause of
Christ and for the Gospel:

> "*For* whoever would save his life
> will lose it,
> and whoever loses his life
> for my sake and the sake of the good news
> will save it.
>
> "*For* what good does it do
> to gain the whole world
> yet forfeit your life?
>
> "*For* what would you give
> in exchange for your life?
>
> "[*For*] anyone in this adulterous and sinful generation
> who is ashamed of me and my words,
> of him will the Son of Man also be ashamed
> when he comes in the glory of his Father
> with the holy angels" (Mk 8:35–38).

"To save your own life" means to keep it, to conserve it.
"To lose it" means, on the contrary, to be incapable of
maintaining it, to allow it to fall into the hands of death.
The two affirmations unfold in an eschatological perspective: they comprise and come from definitive truth, the
judgment of God. But why is it that one who wants to save

one's life will lose it in the final judgment? Because that person trusts only in oneself and does not understand that life is a gift of the Creator, who can save it or send it to ruin beyond the confines of death (cf. Mt 10:28; Lk 12:4ff.).

And why is it that one who renounces his or her own life will save it at the final judgment? Because, vice versa, that person trusts completely in God, the Lord of life and death, the God of the living (cf. Mk 12:27). Jesus speaks as one who is wise: every gain is useless when it comes to the loss of life: "For what will it profit them to gain the whole world and forfeit their life?"

At the base of this conviction, we notice an echo of Psalm 49. Those who trust in themselves, who try to obtain for themselves security based on riches, are headed for destruction. Their shepherd will be death:

> For the ransom of life is costly,
> and can never suffice,
> that one should live on forever
> and never see the grave....
> Like sheep they are appointed for Sheol;
> Death shall be their shepherd;
> straight to the grave they descend,
> and their form shall waste away;
> Sheol shall be their home.
> But God will ransom my soul from the power of Sheol,
> for he will receive me (Ps 49:8–9, 14–15).

The following of Jesus Christ is based on entrusting oneself totally to the Father, the one guarantee of life. Such faith gives one the courage to resist wealth.

And he went away sad

Toward the end of the section dedicated to the following of Jesus, Mark offers an eloquent example of how strong the temptation of wealth is and how difficult it is to offer resistance. The passage is known as "the call of the rich young man," even if the evangelist doesn't really describe him as "young":

> As [Jesus] was setting out on the road a man ran up and knelt before him. "Good Teacher," he asked, "what should I do to gain eternal life?"
>
> Jesus said to him, "Why do you call me good? No one is good but God alone. You know the commandments, 'You shall not murder, you shall not commit adultery, you shall not steal, do not bear false witness, do not defraud, honor your father and mother.'"
>
> "Teacher," he said, "I have obeyed all these from my youth."
>
> As Jesus gazed upon him he was moved with love for him and said, "One thing is left for you; go sell what you have and give to the poor and you will have treasure in heaven, and come follow me."
>
> But he was shocked by what Jesus had said and went off saddened, because he had many properties (Mk 10:17–22).

There is a strong contrast between the initiative of Jesus, who shows kindness to his interlocutor ("looking at him he loved him"), and the man's response, which is lacking.

The young man has posed, with a certain apprehension, the fundamental ethical question: "What must I do to gain eternal life?" (Mk 10:17)

Jesus' answer directs him to the commandments as the basis of social life, as the way that leads to life. In return, the man affirms that he has observed them "completely" from his youth, that is, from the age of reason. Thus, he may be considered a *just man*. What else is he lacking?

Jesus shows him what he still lacks, one thing only. But before doing so, Jesus displays his affection, almost as if to give this man the courage he will need. What does the "just man" standing before Jesus lack? He lacks treasure in heaven! Something not acquired merely by avoiding what could damage another's life (do not kill, do not commit adultery, do not steal...). One acquires it in a positive way, by doing good, by putting one's own riches at the disposition of the poor.

The young man did not expect this aspect of the "*what more*" and is blocked by his own question: "What must *I* do?" I imagine that at this point he is unable to meet Jesus' loving gaze, that he has lowered his eyes. Jesus tries in vain to capture his attention. The young man remains closed in the fortress of his *ego,* protected by his many riches. But his face is clouded over and his soul has become sad.

Jesus too must have shown traces of regret at the sight of this just man torn in half, who went away sad.

Dialoguing with the Word

The temptation of wealth can also be found in deluding oneself that one's goodness will multiply in proportion to the goods one possesses, that life depends on having:

> Truly, no ransom avails for one's life,
> there is no price one can give to God for it.
> For the ransom of life is costly,
> and can never suffice (Ps 49:7–8).

- • Where do you place your life's security?

- • What value does Christ's understanding of poverty have for you?

- • How do you share with the poor?

- • What do you feel the Lord is asking you to "leave" in order to follow him?

Look, we have left everything

After the rich young man goes away, Jesus looks around, seeking the gaze of his disciples, and he comments:

"My children, how hard it is to enter the Kingdom of God;
it is easier for a camel
to go through a needle's eye
than for a rich man to enter the Kingdom of God!"
(Mk 10:24–25)

The Master uses hyperbole for didactic purposes, in order to explain the effective difficulty of salvation for the rich. The disciples shudder: "Then who can be saved?" Jesus gazes at them once more and adds:

"For men it is impossible,
but not for God!
All things are possible for God" (Mk 10:27).

The dialogue is so transparent that it is easy to imagine the scene and ourselves as part of it. An exchange of looks transpires. The Master's eyes search those of his disciples, almost as if to find in them the answer that the young man has refused to give. But what the Master has offered in that moment is extremely disconcerting for the disciples. Is it even possible then to reach salvation? If the just rich, who are blessed by God, cannot save themselves, who can?

There is need of another reassuring look from Jesus and for his faith in the salvific power of God. Jesus places the salvation of each person, even of the rich, in the hands of God: "All things are possible for God" (cf. Gen 18:14; Job 42:2; Zech 8:6).

Peter, the first called (Mk 1:16), steps in. Here too, as elsewhere, he is the spokesman for the other disciples:

"You see we have *left everything*
and *followed* you" (Mk 10:28).

Jesus' response is quick and consoling. He does not allow himself to be outdone in generosity:

"Amen, I say to you,
there is no one who has left
house or brothers or sisters or mother or father
or children or fields
for my sake and for the sake of the good news,
who will not receive now, in this time, a hundredfold
in houses and brothers and sisters and mothers and fields,
along with persecution,
and in the coming age life eternal" (Mk 10:29–30).

The early Christian community remembered with admiration and gratitude the example of Peter and the other disciples, who had the courage and the strength *to leave everything* in order *to follow* Jesus. Unlike the rich young man, they knew how to say yes to Jesus' demanding call to follow.

Their response is a source of hope and encouragement. Some say no to the demands of the Gospel, but others have said yes. The apostles are faithful to Jesus. Their behavior remains the example for disciples of every Christian generation.

Mark is very concrete. The first disciples did not leave a generic "everything," but an "everything" made up of specific things and people: house, family, property. Perhaps, in itself, their everything was little. But it was and remains their *all*. And it is precisely this point that Peter puts forward with his simple and immediate statement: "Look, we have left *everything*."

It's as if he is saying: *Nothing for us is more important than you. We have placed you before our family, before our possessions and our business. For us, you mean more than anyone or anything.*

The Master's promise is comforting. Impoverished existence for love of him and of the Gospel will already see enrichment in the present: an increase of goods and of people. This alludes to the ecclesial experience: in the community and within the same sharing, the Christian receives a hundredfold in brothers, sisters, and goods. Luke recounts with obvious wonder the experience of the first Christian community:

> All the believers were together and had everything in common, and they used to sell their property and possessions

and distribute it to them all, according to the needs of each individual. By common consent they continued to meet daily in the Temple and at home they broke bread, sharing their food with joy and simplicity of heart, praising God and enjoying the good will of all the people (Acts 2:44–47).

But the Master does not hide the trials and persecutions that always accompany those who want to follow him. All who will know how to welcome this "hundredfold" in suffering will possess eternal *life* with him.

Dialoguing with the Word

Ardent determination is not enough to radically follow Jesus. The courage to leave everything comes from God. One can find it in humble faith and in prayer.

- Prolong your prayer and stir up the fire of your faith in the promise of Jesus, who assures you of the hundredfold.

- Ask for courage and sustenance in adversity resulting from Christian witness and from announcing the Gospel.

CHAPTER SEVEN

Bartimaeus,
Icon of the True Disciple

*T*he account of the blind man from Jericho concludes the great theme of "following." Only Mark precisely identifies the protagonist, "the son of Timaeus," and he does so twice, adding the original Aramaic expression "Bartimaeus." The blind man's healing/vocation story is skillfully placed at the end of the lengthy central section that outlines the conditions for following Jesus (Mk 8:31–10:52).

The entire section unfolds *en tê hodô* ("along the way"). It is precisely along the way from Jericho to Jerusalem that Mark places this striking story.

> Then they came to Jericho.
> When he was leaving
> with both his disciples and a considerable crowd,
> blind Bartimaeus—the son of Timaeus—
> a blind beggar,
> was sitting by the road, begging.
> And when he heard that it was Jesus of Nazareth,
> he began to cry out,

"Jesus, Son of David,
have mercy on me!"
Many of the people were telling him to be quiet,
but he cried out all the more,
"Son of David, have mercy on me!"
Jesus stopped and said,
"Call him!"
They called the blind man and said to him,
"Take courage! Get up! He is calling you!"
So he threw off his cloak,
jumped up, and came to Jesus.
And in answer to him Jesus said,
"What do you want me to do for you?"
The blind man said to him,
"Rabbi, please let me see again!"
Jesus said to him,
"Go your way, your faith has saved you!"
At once he regained his sight
and followed him along the road (Mk 10:46–52).

A play on similarities and connections...

a) ...*with the story of the rich young man.* The beginning of the episode with Bartimaeus is similar to that of the rich young man: "As [Jesus] was setting out on the road" (Mk 10:17); "When [Jesus] was leaving Jericho..." (10:46). The hurry of the two men to meet Jesus is also the same: the rich man "ran up and knelt before him" (Mk 10:17), and Bartimaeus "jumped up" (10:50).

Other elements tie the two stories together by contrast. Jesus asks the rich young man to sell his possessions and then follow him, but the man won't. Bartimaeus, on the contrary, anticipates Jesus' request, spontaneously throwing aside his mantle.... One man goes away sad, the other follows with joy. The rich man does not know how to "leave" in order to follow; Bartimaeus, instead, even though asked to leave, follows Jesus along his way.

One has the distinct impression that Bartimaeus's response makes up for the empty space left by the rich young man. The poor beggar has discovered his vision and, at the same time, the treasure he is not willing to lose: Jesus.

b) ...*with the attitude of the sons of Zebedee*. Also noteworthy is a connection with the episode featuring Zebedee's two sons. In both scenes, Jesus asks the same question: "What do you want me to do for you?" (Mk 10:36; 10:51)

Of relevance here is the fact that these are the only two situations in which such a question occurs in the Gospel of Mark. The request is put forward, however, very differently. The two sons of Zebedee ask to "sit" at the right hand of Christ (i.e., sharing his power), while the blind man jumps to his feet and asks for his sight in order to follow.

c) ...*with the entrance of Jesus in Jerusalem*. The successive text, Jesus' entrance in Jerusalem, connects to the image of the mantle. To go to Jesus who calls him, Bartimaeus throws aside "his mantle" (Mk 10:50); when Jesus enters Jerusalem, many people throw down their mantles on the street before him (11:8).

Dynamics and meaning of the story

Mark describes in detail the protagonist of this story. He confirms the man's identity—he is Bartimaeus, the son of Timaeus—and stresses three aspects about him: he is blind, he is a beggar, and he is seated at the side of the road. A character begins to take shape marked by his circumstances of infirmity (he is blind), poverty (a beggar), and marginalization (seated at "the side" of the street). We picture this poor man huddled beneath his mantle. For a person blind like himself, this mantle represents everything: covering to keep him warm, defense against objects that passersby throw at him, protection from nosey, prying eyes. The mantle covers and shields him. Yet, Bartimaeus will not hesitate to cast it aside.

The concluding scene is in fact diametrically opposite that of the first: Bartimaeus has thrown aside his mantle, can now see, and is walking along the street. What has caused this very dynamic and luminous conclusion?

The evangelist does not say how much Bartimaeus may have known about Jesus, but one thing is clear: he transforms the simple news of Jesus passing by into a confession of faith. "Son of David" is clearly a messianic title. And not only that. To his messianic declaration, Bartimaeus adds the request for help. He knows that he needs the Messiah's mercy, and implores twice: "Jesus, Son of David, have mercy on me" (v. 47); "Son of David, have mercy on me" (v. 48).

Bartimaeus cries out with all the breath he has. The people around Jesus, presumably his disciples, "scold" him (*epetimôn*) and try to shut him up. Is it any wonder that it is the disciples who reprove the poor blind man? In the preceding text, they had "rebuked" the children whom the mothers were bringing to Jesus so that he could bless them (cf. Mk 10:13). In that instance Jesus "was angry" (Mark's Jesus does not hide his true feelings!), and with a certain irritation over his disciples' intolerance, he had added: "Let the children come to me!" (Mk 10:14)

How does Jesus now react in the face of this new intolerance? Mark notes that Jesus "stopped" (*kai stas*). It is a significant detail because, as noted earlier, Mark's Jesus is always on the move. This "stopping" is accompanied by his taking a firm position in favor of Bartimaeus: "Call him!" (v. 49) Jesus could have called the blind man himself, as he did with Zacchaeus (Lk 19:5), but he wants those who were telling Bartimaeus to be quiet to be the ones to call him. He wants his disciples to change their attitude, to realize that they cannot follow him in that way. He did not call them to become his "bodyguards," nor to defend him from the troublesome cries of the poor...but rather to "become fishers of men" (Mk 1:17).

Notice how solicitous they become—these same men who previously were ordering Bartimaeus to be silent. They now direct their attention toward the blind man, telling him: "Take courage! Get up! He is calling you!" (v. 49) By stopping, Jesus has changed their hearts.

Bartimaeus, on his part, does not pay attention to any of this. Immediately he throws aside his cloak and jumps to his feet (v. 50). We can picture him, though rather old and crouched down, suddenly springing to his feet like some eager young man. Our beggar has rediscovered his youth! Then, at last, he stands before Jesus.

Mark notes that Jesus "answered him" (v. 51). This leads us to believe that the Master has already heard Bartimaeus's prayer and now, in response, asks him: "What do you want me to do for you?"

Bartimaeus comes forward promptly with his request, prefacing it with a title full of affection, which Mark records in the original Aramaic: "*Rabbi,* please let me see again!" Seated at the edge of the street, he had cried out at the top of his voice: "Son of David, have mercy on me." Now that he is before Jesus, he calls him *Rabbi,* "my teacher"! He has entered into a close relationship that is not only physical but spiritual. By now, Jesus is "his" Master.

How does Jesus react? Usually, he performs healings by the imposition of hands or a healing word. In the healing of the blind man of Bethsaida, all of this was explained in a very particular way: Jesus had to repeat the therapeutic gesture a second time (Mk 8:25). Instead, with Bartimaeus he does nothing. There is neither gesture nor word. He doesn't need to do anything, because there already exists everything necessary for the miracle to occur. Bartimaeus's faith is such that it brings him salvation: "Go your way; your faith has saved you" (v. 52).

And immediately Bartimaeus "regained his sight and followed him along the road."

Almost as if releasing him from the debt of a gift received, Jesus says to him: "Go your way." But Bartimaeus, who by now has excellent vision, does not go away. He has seen (understood) where his treasure lies. Full of joy, he follows his Master no longer from the outskirts, but down the middle of the street.

In conclusion, Bartimaeus's behavior exemplifies stages in the journey of faith. Three important elements appear:

1) to put into action a faith that invokes: "Jesus, have mercy on me!";

2) to throw aside one's cloak: that is to say, that which could be an impediment to following Jesus, such as attachment to material goods and all that may be closed within ourselves;

3) to follow Jesus on the way that leads to Jerusalem.

These various aspects are helpful in synthesizing the message of Mark's Gospel around a theme of discipleship that, as we have said, embodies Christology. Bartimaeus, the one who could not see, follows "his Master" along the same road, the road that goes up to Jerusalem, where Jesus accomplishes the paschal mystery: the way of the cross and resurrection.

Dialoguing with the Word

The blind Bartimaeus is not content with what he heard being said. Others tell him that Jesus of Nazareth is passing by, and he invokes him as "Son of David." He elaborates the news and transforms it into a profession of faith.

- How is your faith? Are you content to simply mouth what others understand, or do you challenge yourself to deeper personal study and application?

- Are you able to discern "God's passing" in the events of your life and in history?

Bartimaeus combines existential poverty, expressed in the humble invocation "have mercy on me," with a coherent exterior attitude. He throws away his cloak in order to run after Jesus.

- What is the "cloak" that you may be using to "protect" yourself, but that you realize impedes you from freely running after the Lord?

Bartimaeus comes to Jesus because he was invited: "Take courage! Get up! He is calling you!" He is called through the disciples, through the apostolate of the Church.

- How do you relate with those who are "far away," with the marginalized?

- Are you concerned that everyone will find the Lord, or do you resemble those who "scold" the poor blind man?

CHAPTER EIGHT

A Road to Continue

*J*esus is received in Jerusalem as the awaited Messiah. Palms and cloaks are placed on the ground where he passes, while the crowd enthusiastically exclaims: "Blessed is he who comes in the name of the Lord" (Mk 11:9).

But the hosannas last a short time. Enthusiasm quickly gives way to quarrel. In the Temple, a controversy erupts when Jesus overturns the tables of the money changers and the sellers of doves. Debate opens up with the priests, scribes, and elders when Jesus tells the parable of the murderous tenants of the vineyard (Mk 12:1–12). And disagreement further ensues with the Pharisees and the Herodians when Jesus responds: "Render to Caesar the things that are Caesar's, and to God the things that are God's" (12:17).

The Master is decisively in contrast with the rich Sadducees, who mock hope in the resurrection: "You are greatly mistaken" (Mk 12:8–27). And he charges with vain glory those who, like the scribes, love to be treated with marks of respect (cf. 12:38–40).

Where do all these arguments and hostilities lead him? The way of the Son of Man passes through rejection, suffering, and the cross.

The account of the passion represents the culmination of the Gospel according to Mark. It opens with a chronological/liturgical reference: "Two days before the Passover" (Mk 14:1). Against this backdrop rest both the plot of the priests and scribes to kill Jesus and the supper at Bethany. There Jesus' surprising anointing is performed by an anonymous woman, whose gesture causes his supper companions to grow indignant at the waste of so costly a perfume (14:3–9). Judas's plotting with the high priests follows (vv. 10–11).

A second chronological/liturgical indication ("On the first day of Unleavened Bread": Mk 14:12) introduces the Last Supper account, the episodes at Gethsemane, and the other events of the passion. Jesus confronts his destiny alone. He is aware of the gravity of this moment, predicting the betrayal of Judas, the scandal of all his disciples, and Peter's denial. But he announces that he will rise again and will go ahead of them into Galilee (14:27–31).

Before the Sanhedrin and high priest, who question him on the night of the trial, Jesus finally reveals his secret. He declares himself to be the Messiah, the Son of the Blessed One, and with the words of Daniel 7:13 he alludes to his coming glorification. Following the outrage of the high priest, they condemn him to death and mock him.

The mocking of Jesus, king of the Jews, is continued the following morning in the praetorium, after Pilate's condemnation, and it extends right to the foot of the cross. The leaders of the priests and scribes mock him until the end: "Let the Messiah, the King of Israel, come down now from the cross, so we can see and believe" (Mk 15:32)

Then Mark counts the hours: "from the hour of noon until three in the afternoon" (15:33). Three hours of darkness, which Jesus lives in total solitude, feeling abandoned even by the Father. He cries out the first verse of Psalm 22: "My God, my God, why have you abandoned me?" (15:34) Finally, after another indecipherable cry, he dies.

Then two wonders occur. First, the Temple veil—most likely located between the sanctuary and the "Holy of Holies"—is rent in two (*eschisthê*, "was ripped": Mk 15:38) from top to bottom. The sign is interpreted as a confirmation of the Crucified's messianic identity. The Temple prophecy that Jesus pronounced (13:2), and which was hurled at him as an accusation (14:58) and reason for scorn (15:29–30), begins to be fulfilled. It's as if heaven reproves those responsible for the unjust sentence, while Jesus is justified.

I would like to recall, however, that the verb used here (*schizomai*) is the same one that at the beginning of the Gospel indicated what Jesus saw by the River Jordan: "he saw the heavens torn apart" (Mk 1:10). The prophet Isaiah's invocation comes to mind: "Oh, that you would rend the heavens and come down!" I believe that Mark sees here the fulfillment of that ardent invocation. Now the glory of the Eternal has torn open the heavens and the veil of the Temple.

Nearby stands the pagan centurion, who recognizes in the Crucified One the Son of God. Seeing Jesus die in this way, the centurion exclaims: "Truly this man was the Son of God" (Mk 15:39).

Mark ends the account quickly, with three scenes that have women as the protagonists. These women:

— observe his death (15:40–41);

— observe the place where he is buried (15:42–47);

— and receive the announcement of the resurrection (16:1–8).

Like a flashback, the first of these three scenes summarizes the complex pattern of the entire account: Galilee, the journey, Jerusalem. The women, who from a certain distance observe the Messiah's death (Mk 15:40–41), are those who "follow" (*êkolouthoun*) him to Galilee. Three are mentioned by name (the same three whom we find again on Easter morning): Mary Magdalene, Mary the mother of James the younger and of Joses, and Salome. With them are "many other women who had come up with him to Jerusalem" (15:40–41).

If before his execution it was men who had followed Jesus and played a part, after his execution it was women who did so. In the first and second scenes, they appear as mute spectators, limiting themselves "to observing" (vv. 40, 47). In the third scene, instead, they make their entrance with a question: "Who will roll the stone away from the door of the tomb for us?" (Mk 16:3), and they exit it distressed, with embarrassing silence (16:8).

The great Easter announcement is reserved to a young man dressed in white and seated at the right of the sepulcher. He addresses Mary Magdalene, Mary the mother of James, and Salome:

"You are looking for Jesus the Nazarene who was crucified. He is risen, he is not here."

He then entrusts them with a message:

"But go tell his disciples and Peter: he is going ahead of you into Galilee. You will see him there, just as he told you."

And once again, Jesus is he who *goes before*: "He is going ahead of you into Galilee; there you will see him."

How? When? Mark doesn't say. He leaves us with a provocative silence. The account is finished, and the journey opens up before the believer who will follow in the footsteps of Christ.

Dialoguing with the Word

• Have the courage to begin again. Return symbolically to Galilee, where Jesus has called you. At this point nothing will be like it was before. The heavens are opened also for you. This Son of Man nailed to a cross has spoken the supreme word about the love of God, as the Apostle Paul well understood:

For the message of the cross...for those who are being saved—for us...is the power of God. For it is written: "I will destroy the wisdom of the wise, and the insights of the intelligent I will reject." Where is the wise man?

Where is the scribe? Where is the skilled debater of this age? Has God not turned the wisdom of this world to foolishness? For since, in God's wisdom, the world was unable to come to knowledge of God with its own wisdom, God chose through the foolishness of our proclamation to save those who believe. Jews ask for signs and Greeks look for wisdom, but we proclaim Christ crucified—a stumbling block for Jews and foolishness to Greeks, but for those who have been chosen, both Jew and Greek, Christ the power of God and the wisdom of God, for God's foolishness is wiser than human wisdom, and God's weakness is stronger than human strength (1 Cor 1:18–25).

- Take the risk of believing. Follow the Master on the way of the cross, and *you will see him risen* in your own life.

BOOKS & MEDIA

The Daughters of St. Paul operate book and media centers at the following addresses. Visit, call or write the one nearest you today, or find us on the World Wide Web, www.pauline.org

CALIFORNIA
3908 Sepulveda Blvd, Culver City, CA 90230   310-397-8676
2650 Broadway Street, Redwood City, CA 94063   650-369-4230
5945 Balboa Avenue, San Diego, CA 92111   858-565-9181

FLORIDA
145 S.W. 107th Avenue, Miami, FL 33174   305-559-6715

HAWAII
1143 Bishop Street, Honolulu, HI 96813   808-521-2731
Neighbor Islands call: 866-521-2731

ILLINOIS
172 North Michigan Avenue, Chicago, IL 60601   312-346-4228

LOUISIANA
4403 Veterans Memorial Blvd, Metairie, LA 70006   504-887-7631

MASSACHUSETTS
885 Providence Hwy, Dedham, MA 02026   781-326-5385

MISSOURI
9804 Watson Road, St. Louis, MO 63126   314-965-3512

NEW JERSEY
561 U.S. Route 1, Wick Plaza, Edison, NJ 08817   732-572-1200

NEW YORK
150 East 52nd Street, New York, NY 10022   212-754-1110

PENNSYLVANIA
9171-A Roosevelt Blvd, Philadelphia, PA 19114   215-676-9494

SOUTH CAROLINA
243 King Street, Charleston, SC 29401   843-577-0175

TENNESSEE
4811 Poplar Avenue, Memphis, TN 38117   901-761-2987

TEXAS
114 Main Plaza, San Antonio, TX 78205   210-224-8101

VIRGINIA
1025 King Street, Alexandria, VA 22314   703-549-3806

CANADA
3022 Dufferin Street, Toronto, ON M6B 3T5   416-781-9131